STERLING BIOGRAPHIES

GERONIMO

Apache Renegade

George Sullivan

STERLING

New York / London
www.sterlingpublishing.com/kids

STERLING and the distinctive Sterling logo are registered trademarks of
Sterling Publishing Co., Inc.

Library of Congress Cataloging-in-Publication Data
Sullivan, George, 1927–
  Geronimo : Apache renegade / by George Sullivan.
    p. cm. — (Sterling biographies)
  Includes bibliographical references and index.
  ISBN 978-1-4027-6279-6 (pbk.) — ISBN 978-1-4027-6843-9 (hardcover) 1. Geronimo, 1829–
1909—Juvenile literature. 2. Apache Indians—Biography—Juvenile literature.
3. Apache Indians—Wars—Juvenile literature. I. Title.
  E99.A6G32745 2010
  970.004'97—dc22
  [B]

                                                                                    2009024135

Lot #: 10 9 8 7 6 5 4 3 2
01/11

Published by Sterling Publishing Co., Inc.
387 Park Avenue South, New York, NY 10016
© 2010 by George Sullivan

Distributed in Canada by Sterling Publishing
c/o Canadian Manda Group, 165 Dufferin Street
Toronto, Ontario, Canada M6K 3H6
Distributed in the United Kingdom by GMC Distribution Services
Castle Place, 166 High Street, Lewes, East Sussex, England BN7 1XU
Distributed in Australia by Capricorn Link (Australia) Pty. Ltd.
P.O. Box 704, Windsor, NSW 2756, Australia

Printed in China
All rights reserved

Sterling ISBN 978-1-4027-6279-6 (paperback)
          ISBN 978-1-4027-6843-9 (hardcover)

Image research by Larry Schwartz

For information about custom editions, special sales, premium and corporate
purchases, please contact Sterling Special Sales Department at 800-805-5489
or specialsales@sterlingpublishing.com.

Contents

Events in the Life of Geronimo

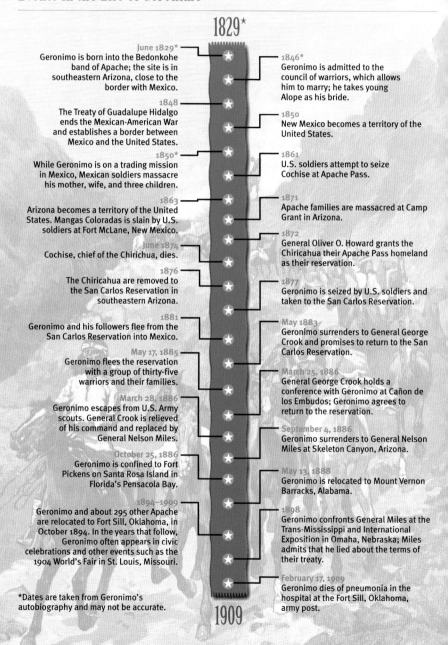

1829*

June 1829*
Geronimo is born into the Bedonkohe band of Apache; the site is in southeastern Arizona, close to the border with Mexico.

1846*
Geronimo is admitted to the council of warriors, which allows him to marry; he takes young Alope as his bride.

1848
The Treaty of Guadalupe Hidalgo ends the Mexican-American War and establishes a border between Mexico and the United States.

1850
New Mexico becomes a territory of the United States.

1850*
While Geronimo is on a trading mission in Mexico, Mexican soldiers massacre his mother, wife, and three children.

1861
U.S. soldiers attempt to seize Cochise at Apache Pass.

1863
Arizona becomes a territory of the United States. Mangas Coloradas is slain by U.S. soldiers at Fort McLane, New Mexico.

1871
Apache families are massacred at Camp Grant in Arizona.

June 1874
Cochise, chief of the Chirichua, dies.

1872
General Oliver O. Howard grants the Chiricahua their Apache Pass homeland as their reservation.

1876
The Chiricahua are removed to the San Carlos Reservation in southeastern Arizona.

1877
Geronimo is seized by U.S. soldiers and taken to the San Carlos Reservation.

1881
Geronimo and his followers flee from the San Carlos Reservation into Mexico.

May 1883
Geronimo surrenders to General George Crook and promises to return to the San Carlos Reservation.

May 17, 1885
Geronimo flees the reservation with a group of thirty-five warriors and their families.

March 25, 1886
General George Crook holds a conference with Geronimo at Cañon de los Embudos; Geronimo agrees to return to the reservation.

March 28, 1886
Geronimo escapes from U.S. Army scouts. General Crook is relieved of his command and replaced by General Nelson Miles.

September 4, 1886
Geronimo surrenders to General Nelson Miles at Skeleton Canyon, Arizona.

October 25, 1886
Geronimo is confined to Fort Pickens on Santa Rosa Island in Florida's Pensola Bay.

May 13, 1888
Geronimo is relocated to Mount Vernon Barracks, Alabama.

1894–1909
Geronimo and about 295 other Apache are relocated to Fort Sill, Oklahoma, in October 1894. In the years that follow, Geronimo often appears in civic celebrations and other events such as the 1904 World's Fair in St. Louis, Missouri.

1898
Geronimo confronts General Miles at the Trans-Mississippi and International Exposition in Omaha, Nebraska; Miles admits that he lied about the terms of their treaty.

*Dates are taken from Geronimo's autobiography and may not be accurate.

February 17, 1909
Geronimo dies of pneumonia in the hospital at the Fort Sill, Oklahoma, army post.

1909

Full of Vengeance

I could not call back my loved ones, I could not bring back the dead Apaches, but I could rejoice in this revenge.

Geronimo, a young Apache at the time, set out one day with his family from their homeland, in what is now southeastern Arizona, on a trading mission into Mexico. Many other families went with him. In Mexico, they camped near the town of Janos, which the Apache called Kas-ki-yeh.

The men went into town to trade each day, leaving their families behind. On this fateful evening, they returned home to find that Mexican soldiers had viciously attacked their camp. They had massacred their women and children and stolen their ponies and supplies. The dead were strewn everywhere. Geronimo's wife, three children, and his mother were among those slaughtered. He found their bodies lying in a pool of blood.

"I had lost all," Geronimo said.

A year later, the Apache returned to Janos with revenge on their minds. Led by Geronimo, the warriors attacked an encampment of Mexican soldiers. The battle lasted two hours. The Apache's victory was complete—no soldier survived.

While the other Apache were satisfied with the pain and punishment they had dealt the Mexicans, Geronimo was not. His heart was filled with hatred, and he would spend a lifetime pursuing vengeance for all that he and his people had lost.

CHAPTER 1

Apache Boyhood

This range was our fatherland; among these mountains our wigwams were hidden; . . . the rocky caverns were our burial places.

Geronimo's name is usually linked to tales of violence and even savagery. But his early life was calm and peaceful. He was born an Apache, the name used to describe any one of several American Indian tribal groups of the southwestern United States. The Apache were known to be gentle and affectionate toward members of their own tribe, especially their children.

Geronimo said that he was born in 1829. But most historians question this date, and no one has been able to provide a date with any certainty. It is more likely that Geronimo was born in the early 1820s, and he is believed to have been born "near the headwaters of the Gila River in what is now southeastern Arizona." The site is near the present town of Clifton, which is about ten miles west of Arizona's border with New Mexico. It was and still is an area of great physical beauty, with deep, steep-sided valleys and vast forests of ponderosa pine. These woodlands are home to

Geronimo said he was born near the headwaters of the Gila River in southwestern Arizona, pictured here in a modern photograph.

Geronimo, the Storyteller

For most Native Americans of the American West, there were no written records. All history was transmitted by speech. However, Geronimo was an exception. The Indian leader provided a revealing record of his life and the Apache wars. Published as a book, it is titled *Geronimo: His Own Story*.

As a man in his eighties, in 1905 and 1906, Geronimo dictated his life story through a translator and a transcriber. Asa (Ace) Daklugie, Geronimo's cousin, served as a translator. He converted the Apache language that Geronimo spoke into English. Stephen Barrett, then superintendent of schools in Lawton, Oklahoma, transcribed, wrote down, what Daklugie said.

Not all historians are happy with the results. They say Geronimo wasn't always accurate. Some dates are wrong. Some events involving raiding and killing by the Apache have been left out.

Even though there may be flaws in Geronimo's version of events, it still provides valuable insights into Geronimo's life as well as a rare view of the customs and beliefs of the Apache.

Geronimo's account of his life represents the work of three people: Asa Daklugie (right), who served as his translator, Geronimo himself (center), and Stephen Barrett (left), who wrote down Geronimo's words as spoken in English by Daklugie.

black bears, elk, deer, and wild turkeys. Countless hot springs flank the rivers.

Geronimo's father was called *Taklishim*, which meant "The Gray One." His mother, an Apache, was called Juana—a Spanish name she may have gotten by being captured and enslaved by the Spanish.

Geronimo said that he was "fourth in a family of eight children—four boys and four girls." But the Apache did not distinguish cousins from brothers and sisters. To them, they were all the same. A family of eight would have been extremely rare among the Apache. It is more likely that Geronimo had one actual sister, as we know the term today.

As an infant, Geronimo was given the name *Goyahkla*, which means "one who yawns." The name Geronimo came later, during a conflict with Mexicans in the late 1850s. "As a babe I rolled on the dirt floor of my father's **tepee**, hung in my **tosch** at my mother's back or suspended from the bough of a tree. I was warmed by the sun, rocked by the winds, and sheltered by the trees as other Indian babes," he later remembered.

This 1903 photograph depicts the type of cradleboard, or *tosch*, in which Apache infants rested, slept, and were carried.

Play and Work

Goyahkla played with his brothers and sisters. As Geronimo once recalled, "Sometimes we played at hide-and-seek among the rocks and pines; sometimes we loitered in the shade of the cottonwood trees or sought the *shudock* [the wild cherry tree],

Like Goyahkla's mother, other Native American women labored in the fields while carrying a child strapped to their backs, as shown in this 1906 photograph.

while our parents worked in the field. . . . Sometimes we would hide away from our mother to see if she could find us, and often when thus concealed go to sleep and perhaps remain hidden for many hours."

Boys and girls would sometimes sneak away and meet at a place miles from their campsite. There they would play all day. They were never punished for this behavior. But if their hiding place was discovered, they were made fun of, as it showed lack of skill and cunning to hide successfully.

As teenagers, Apache children toiled in the family fields. As an adult, Geronimo reminisced, "When the crops were to be planted we broke the ground with wooden hoes . . . [and] planted the corn in straight rows, the beans among the corn, and the melons and pumpkins in irregular order over the field."

Apache did not grow tobacco; it grew wild. Most, if not all American Indians smoked, both men and women. Geronimo later described, "No boy was allowed to smoke until they had hunted alone and killed some large game—wolves or bears. Unmarried women were not prohibited from smoking, but were considered immodest if they did so."

From his mother, Goyahkla learned the tribal origins of his people. She taught him to pray to *Usen*, the supreme being of the Apache, "for strength, health, wisdom, and protection."

The Apache Nation

As a nation, the Apache ranged south from much of New Mexico and eastern Arizona and into vast stretches of Texas and Mexico. They also extended north out of New Mexico into southeastern Colorado. By occupying these lands, they had to deal with one set of invaders after another, including the Spanish, Mexicans, and Americans. A Spanish expedition led by Francisco Vásquez de Coronado arrived around 1540 and hostilities started soon after. During the same era, the Apache were engaged in conflicts with the Mexicans for long stretches of time. Pioneering Americans presented an ever-growing threat beginning in the 1850s.

The Apache nation that confronted these unwelcome arrivals was made up of several regional groups. These included the Mescalero, Jicarilla, Lipan, Kiowa, Chiricahua, and Western Apache. Goyahkla belonged to an Apache band called the Bedonkohe, a subdivision of the Chiricahua. Bedonkohe warriors traveled together with another Chiricahua band called the Warm Springs Apache and lived in the Mogollon Mountains near the present Arizona–New Mexico border.

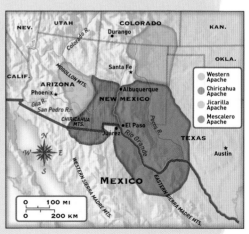

This map depicts the homelands of the principal Apache groups in the southwestern United States and northern Mexico.

Compared to most of their enemies, the Apache were small in stature. And in virtually every conflict, they were outnumbered. But when it came to toughness, no enemy was their equal.

Warrior Training

When Goyahkla began training in raiding and warfare, his tutor said to him: "My son, you know no one will help you in this world. . . . No one is your friend, not even your sister, your father, or your mother. Your legs are your friends; your brain is your friend; your eyesight is your friend; your hair is your friend; your hands are your friends; you must do something with them." To develop his "friends," Goyahkla was taught to shoot a bow and arrow as soon as he was strong enough. When he was eight or nine years old, he joined groups of Bedonkohe men on

As a young boy, Goyahkla received instruction on the use of a bow and arrow, much like the young Native American boy in this photograph from 1900.

It took great skill for a young hunter like Goyahkla to stalk a deer. Such an event is seen in this depiction of Henry Wadsworth Longfellow's "The Song of Hiawatha."

hunting expeditions. They sought deer, antelope, buffalo, elk, and wild turkey.

To the young hunter Goyahkla, "It required more skill to hunt the deer than any other animal." He was taught to always approach a deer against the wind so that the deer wouldn't smell him coming. Concealed by the growth of bushes and shrubs, he would crawl along the ground toward a group of grazing deer. When he got close, he would strike with an arrow or a spear.

The deer was more valuable to the Apache than any other animal. The flesh was dried and stored away for future use. The hair was removed from the deer's hide, which was then softened and used to make moccasins and clothing.

Rabbits were hunted on horseback. Goyahkla would chase a rabbit at full gallop. As he drew near, he would lean over and strike the rabbit with a hunting club. This provided great sport for young boys, but as warriors, they seldom hunted small game. Goyahkla hunted bears with a spear and killed several mountain lions with a bow and arrows. He would then carry the big game home on his horse.

The mountain streams were filled with fish, but the Apache did not try to catch them. They were taught that fish was not acceptable as food and that "Usen did not intend snakes, frogs, or fishes to be eaten." As a man, Goyahkla said he had "never eaten of them."

Boyhood's End

When Goyahkla was still a young boy, his father was sick for a long time and eventually died. Friends and relatives dressed the old man in his best clothes, painted his face, and wrapped a cherished blanket around him. The body of Goyahkla's father was taken by his favorite horse to a cave in the mountains. After the body was placed on the floor of the cave with his bows, arrows, and spears, the cave entrance was then sealed with rocks. The grave was hidden by piles of stone. Only his family and close friends knew its location.

After his father's death, Goyahkla began supporting his mother. It was the custom among the Apache for a widow to return to her people where she could be given away or sold by her father or brothers. But his mother "chose to live with [him] and she never desired to marry again."

CHAPTER 2

A Shocking Loss

I was never again contented in our quiet home. . . .
Whenever I . . . saw anything to remind me of
former happy days, my heart would ache for
revenge upon Mexico.

Although he was born and raised during a mostly peaceful time, Goyahkla and other young Apache boys were still made to endure harsh physical training to prepare them for combat. A boy was required to rise before dawn and run up the slope of a nearby mountain. As he ran, he carried a mouthful of water. He could not spit it out until he returned. This exercise was designed to train him to breathe properly through his nose as he ran.

Bedonkohe boys took part in wrestling matches to become skilled in hand-to-hand fighting. They battled one another in slingshot wars, which could result in a broken bone or a blinded eye.

Girls were trained to be strong and vigorous, too. They rose early and, like the boys, were ordered to run long distances. They gathered

Apache women had many chores. One was weaving serviceable baskets. In this undated photograph, a Native American woman and a young child weave baskets together.

firewood, carried water from the streams to the camp, and made clothing from **buckskin**. They learned to weave baskets and construct the family tepee.

Rules of Survival

As he got older, Goyahkla was taught how to live in the wild. He was provided with a week's supply of food—chiefly dried meat, berries, and nuts—and sent out to travel across the open land until he reached the mountains. He moved about only under the cover of darkness. During daylight hours, he concealed himself in the brush. He was taught to locate water holes by climbing to a high place and looking for green spots below. But he would never go to a water hole during the day—only at night.

Never sleep under a tree, he was told, because that is the first place an enemy will look. Instead, Goyahkla was taught to pick out a place in the open to sleep, and to conceal himself in the brush. If he became lost and needed help, he was told to build a fire and send up a smoke signal. But he should put out the fire quickly, then run to a place where he can watch and see whether anyone comes.

When Goyahkla turned seventeen in 1846, he was granted membership in his tribe's council of warriors—a status that thrilled him. Now he was free to go wherever he wanted and to do whatever

This undated lithograph pictures American Indians using signal fires to communicate over long distances.

This engraving from the 19th century depicts American Indians in a tribal conference. As a member of the council of warriors, Goyahkla would attend such meetings.

he liked. Being a council member also meant he could go on the warpath with other members of his tribe. "This would be glorious," he said. "I hoped soon to serve my people in battle. I had long desired to fight with our warriors."

His advance in status also meant that Goyahkla was now free to marry. His choice was a slender, delicate girl named Alope, who was a member of the Nednai, an Apache tribe closely associated with the Bedonkohe.

Marriage Dealings

As soon as he was admitted to the council of warriors, Goyahkla went to Alope's father to tell him of his desire to marry his daughter. According to tribal custom, a financial settlement had to be made. The parents of the boy and girl usually conducted these negotiations. The fact that Goyahkla preferred to handle the arrangements by himself, without advice from his mother, showed his independent nature.

Alope's father asked Goyahkla for "many ponies" in exchange for his daughter. Goyahkla accepted the request without comment. A few days later, he returned with a herd of ponies. As soon as the ponies were presented to Alope's father, she was considered Goyahkla's wife. That "was all the marriage ceremony necessary." But how did Goyahkla acquire the ponies? It is likely he raided a Mexican ranch for them. No one asked, and Goyahkla never told.

Goyahkla declined to live with his first wife in a wickiup, the traditional Apache dwelling, in favor of a tepee, similar to the one pictured here in a photograph taken on the Mescalero Apache Reservation in 1915.

Once married, Goyahkla wanted a new house, and he built a new tepee not far from where his mother lived. Alope adorned the tepee with bear robes and the skins of mountain lions, as well as Goyahkla's spears, bows, and arrows. She strung beads and drew pictures on the buckskin walls as decoration. Meals were cooked in a fire pit, and the smoke was released through a hole in the roof. Goyahkla described Alope as a "good wife" but said "she was never [physically] strong." The couple had three children that "played, loitered, and worked" as Goyahkla had done.

Friction and Strife

During the early years of Goyahkla's marriage, the Bedonkohe were usually at peace with the neighboring Apache tribes as well as the Mexicans who lived to the south. Often, the Indians traded with the Mexicans, exchanging animal skins and furs for knives, ornaments, and brightly colored cloth.

But there was a long history of hostilities between the two groups. After the Spanish arrived in Mexico early in the sixteenth century, they sent Mexicans into Apache territory on slave-hunting expeditions. Then, under Mangas Coloradas, the Bedonkohe's bold leader, the Apache answered with violence of their own. From their tribal hideaways high in the mountains, the Apache raided Mexican ranches and pack trains that were returning to their homeland with herds of horses or cattle and packs bulging with food, clothing, and other supplies. Many Mexicans were killed and wounded in these raids.

In an effort to halt the raids, the Mexican state of Sonora passed a law offering one hundred pesos for every scalp of an Apache warrior, which was a lot of money at the time. Later, the state of Chihuahua made a similar offer.

It was against this troublesome background that Mangas Coloradas, Goyahkla, and other members of the Bedonkohe tribe set out on a trading expedition into Mexico in the summer of 1850. There had been a temporary pause in hostilities, and it looked to be a peaceable trip, so the Bedonkohe women and children went along. Their destination was Janos in the Mexican state of Chihuahua. Just before reaching the town, the group stopped and made camp. Each morning, Goyahkla and the other men would leave their families and go into Janos to trade, leaving just a few men behind as guards.

Family Tragedy

Late one afternoon, as Goyahkla and the other men were returning to their camp, they were met by a group of distressed Apache women. The women blurted out the news that a band of

Mangas Coloradas (1795–1863)

At the time Goyahkla became a member of his tribe's council of warriors, the Bedonkohe were led by Mangas Coloradas. His name meant "Red Sleeves," and he was greatly admired by the Apache people. Many of the white settlers who were to occupy the area also regarded him as a great Indian leader.

Mangas Coloradas looked like a leader. More than six feet tall, he towered over the other Apache. He had a thickly muscled body and an enormous head. Not only was he adept at guiding and directing his band of Apache, but he was also highly skilled as a negotiator when dealing with other tribes.

While in his twenties, Mangas Coloradas captured a young Mexican woman and made her his wife. They had three children. To strengthen his relationships with other Apache groups, he married one of his daughters to the leader of the Western Apache, another to the chief of the Navajo, and the third to Cochise, who became one of the most famous of all Indian chieftains.

Mangas Coloradas, depicted here in a hand-colored engraving from 1886, was the much admired and respected leader of the Bedonkohe Apache.

Mexican troops had attacked the Apache camp and had captured its ponies, stolen its arms, destroyed its supplies, and had murdered Apache women and children.

Stunned by the news, Goyahkla and the other men quickly scattered to evade possible harm and concealed themselves until darkness fell. Then they slipped into the camp one by one. What they found shocked and saddened them. The camp was a shambles, with bodies of young children and women strewn about. Goyahkla had suffered the greatest loss. He discovered his mother, his young wife, and their three children lying in a pool of blood. Other men had suffered heavy losses, too. They were almost crazy with grief.

Goyahkla turned away from the scene and went to stand silently by the river. How long he stood there, he could never recall. His long silence was broken by a comrade who came to tell him that the warriors had called for a council.

At the council meeting, Goyahkla kept his head bowed and watched the proceedings in silence. He and others of the band were well aware that they were without arms, horses, or supplies. They knew they were deep in Mexican territory and surrounded by Mexicans. They thus fully realized that anything but a retreat would be foolish. Mangas Coloradas gave the order for the band to set out for the Mexican–U.S. border and their homes on foot. They were to leave the dead behind. Goyahkla felt he had no purpose left in life. "I finally followed the tribe silently, keeping within hearing distance of the soft noise of the feet of the retreating Apaches."

For several days, Goyahkla and the other men made their way north, stopping only for meals. At the border, they rested for two days. For the first time, Goyahkla spoke with some of the men whose family members had been killed in the massacre. Although they had lost loved ones as well, Goyahkla "had lost all."

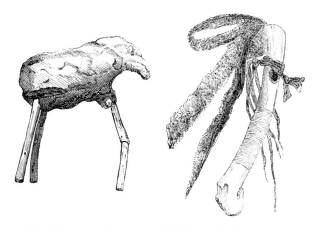

In his grief, Goyahkla destroyed everything that belonged to his murdered family, including his children's toys, similar to the ones shown here—a clay horse and bone whistle that were created by the Indians of the Great Plains.

Back at their settlement, Goyahkla followed the Apache custom of destroying all evidence of those he had lost. He burned the decorations that Alope had made, and the playthings of their children. "I burned them all, even our tepee. I also burned my mother's tepee and destroyed all her property. I was never again contented in our quiet home." Goyahkla vowed vengeance upon the Mexican troopers who had wronged him, and "whenever I . . . saw anything to remind me of former happy days my heart would ache for revenge upon Mexico."

"No Gun Can Ever Kill You"

The great tragedy that Goyahkla suffered had at least one benefit. Through the experience, he received a special gift, or "Power." One day as he was sitting alone with his head bowed, and weeping, he heard a voice calling his name, "Goyahkla!" The voice repeated the name four times. (Four was a magical number to the Apache.) Then Goyahkla heard the voice utter these words:

"No gun can ever kill you. I will take the bullets from the guns of the Mexicans, so they will have nothing but powder. And I will guide your arrows."

In the years that followed, Goyahkla believed that he carried the "Power" with him. In battle, he often acted in a reckless way, putting his life in peril. He was often wounded but always managed to escape a fatal bullet. His good fortune helped to strengthen his belief that he had been endowed with a magical gift.

. . . Goyahkla believed that he carried the "Power" with him.

As soon as the Bedonkohe had gotten a new supply of weapons, Mangas Coloradas held a meeting of tribal warriors. He found that they were of one mind in their eagerness to take the warpath against Mexico to revenge the massacre at Janos.

Goyahkla was sent to obtain the help of other tribes. He first went to the Chiricahua Apache. Cochise, their chief, called a council into session and invited Goyahkla to speak. "You are my relatives—uncles, cousins, brothers," Goyahkla began. "We are men the same as the Mexicans are—we can do to them what they have done to us. I will fight in the front of the battle—I only ask you to follow to avenge this wrong done by these Mexicans."

The Chiricahua under Cochise agreed to ally themselves with the Bedonkohe. Two other tribes, the Mimbreno, also headed by Mangas Coloradas, and the Nednai Apache, under their leader Juh, also joined the campaign.

Seeking Vengeance

In 1851, almost a year from the date of the slaughter, the tribes set out for Janos again. The men painted their faces and

In 1903, artist Charles Craig painted this scene of mounted Apache tribesmen going to war, adorned with feathers and face paint.

fastened war bands—two-inch strips of buckskin—about their foreheads. On their march, they covered forty to forty-five miles a day, pausing only to hide their families in the tall mountains near the Mexican border.

When the war party neared Janos, the men stopped to set up a camp. The Mexicans were aware of their arrival, and eight of them rode out to talk with the Apache. The Indians were in no mood for conversation. Before the Mexicans had a chance to speak, the Indians pounced upon them, quickly killing and scalping all eight.

Goyahkla and others knew that their brutal act would draw the main Mexican military force into battle. And they were right. At mid-morning the following day, the Indians sighted a great mass of armed Mexicans making their way toward the Indian camp. Some were foot soldiers; others were ready to fight on horseback. Because Goyahkla had suffered the greatest loss in the massacre, he was chosen to lead the warriors.

When it came to warfare, Indians generally ambushed their enemies, attacking from behind rocks or brush. But this time, Goyahkla was in no mood for deception. When the Mexicans halted and opened fire, he ordered a frontal attack and led the charge. He fought savagely, piercing one body after another with his long-shafted spear. The fighting lasted almost two hours. "In all the battle I thought of my murdered mother, wife, and babies . . . and I fought with fury," Goyahkla later said.

In the end, Goyahkla and three other warriors stood in the center of the battlefield. Their arrows were gone. Their spears had been broken off in the bodies of the enemy soldiers. A soldier wielding a heavy, sharp-edged sword rushed up to Goyahkla. The two men grappled, and Goyahkla plunged his broken spear into the man, who dropped. When a second soldier charged Goyahkla, the revengeful warrior used the first man's sword to slay him. He then looked about for other Mexican soldiers to kill. There were none. A fierce Apache war whoop rang out over the bloody field.

In the years after, the story of the battle would be told and retold by the Indians, always with great pride. It would be looked upon as one of the greatest of all Apache victories. It was during this great victory that Mexican soldiers bestowed the name of Geronimo on Goyahkla, but historians fail to agree why he was so named.

The Apache had wreaked their vengeance for the massacre at Janos. "I could not call back my loved ones," said Geronimo. "I could not bring back the dead Apache, but I could rejoice in this revenge."

CHAPTER 3

Trouble at Apache Pass

I have killed many Mexicans; I do not know how many, for frequently I did not count them. Some of them were not worth counting.

In the years after the slaughter at Janos, Geronimo continued to lead raids into Mexican territory. As many as twenty or twenty-five other warriors would go with him. When they were successful, they would return with horses, mules, or herds of cattle. Sometimes their plunder also included blankets and food supplies, such as sugar and cheese. After one very successful raid, the warriors called the whole tribe together and feasted for the entire day. They gave presents to everyone, and at night they danced until the next day. Usually only people of the Bedonkohe tribe danced, but sometimes neighboring tribes would be invited. The singing of warriors furnished the music for the dancing. No words were sung, only musical tones.

Renowned American painter and illustrator Frederic Remington created this dramatic painting, which depicts Geronimo and his band returning with stolen horses after a raid in Mexico.

In retaliation for the crushing losses they suffered at Janos, Mexican troops attacked Apache settlements north of the border, burning tepees and taking ponies and weapons. Each side continued to attack the other. But some of the raids led by Geronimo ended in failure. Once in Mexico, the Indians would sometimes meet with troops who had the firepower to overwhelm them. Members of the raiding party would be killed, wounded, or taken prisoner.

A New Era of Expansion

While conflicts with Mexicans occupied the first decades of Geronimo's life as a warrior, that scenario changed during the 1850s. What triggered the change was the Mexican-American War that raged from 1846 into 1848. The Treaty of Guadalupe Hidalgo ended the war on February 2, 1848. Out of that treaty, the United States acquired most of what is now the American Southwest.

The Battle of Buena Vista, shown above in a print from Currier & Ives, was a major battle fought and won by the Americans in February 1847, during the Mexican-American War.

In 1850, Congress created the New Mexico Territory, which included the present states of New Mexico and Arizona. It also included southern Colorado. In 1863, Congress sliced off half of the New Mexico Territory to form the Arizona Territory. Earlier, Texas, after several years as an independent republic, had been admitted to the union as a state in 1845, expanding U.S. lands even farther.

These moves brought into existence a borderline that separated the United States from the Republic of Mexico. The United States was north of the line. Mexico was south of it.

The fast growth and development of the United States from the Atlantic seaboard to the Pacific Ocean resulted, at least in part, from the Americans' sense of mission that such expansion had to happen. Nothing could stop it. "Manifest Destiny" was the term used to express this idea. In their expansionist attitude, most Americans had little respect for the rights or culture of the Indian tribes they encountered. They simply wanted the land. Of course,

In 1872, New York artist John Gast painted this tribute to western expansion, which depicts fearless pioneers, marching toward the frontier. The woman represents Manifest Destiny.

some people understood the injustice of this attitude. But even they believed that the Indians must submit to the advance of white settlement.

Encounter with the Whites

Geronimo's first sight of the American intruders is likely to have taken place around 1851, when he was told that white men were measuring land just to the south of their settlement. He and a group of warriors wasted no time in going to investigate.

After observing them for a time, the Apache went up to the strangers. "We could not understand them very well for we had no interpreter," Geronimo said, "but we made a treaty with them by shaking hands and promising to be brothers."

After the Indians had made camp, the whites came to trade with them. In exchange for shirts and food, the Indians offered the whites buckskins, blankets, and ponies. The Indians also gave the whites some game they had shot. In return, they received

White traders were some of the first people to encounter Native Americans. In a print that dates to about 1900, an Indian couple is pictured doing business with a trader.

money. The Indians looked at the coins and bills in wonderment. They did not know their value. They did not know what to do with them. They later learned from some Navajo tribesmen that what they had been given could be used as a medium of exchange.

Geronimo and the others continued to watch the whites as they measured the land. He felt at that time that "they were good men, and we were sorry when they had gone into the west." Peaceful relations between the Indians and white settlers in the Southwest continued for a number of years. This was partly because there were so few settlers. But as the number of whites increased, friendships began to be severely tested.

Peaceful relations between the Indians and white settlers in the Southwest continued for a number of years.

A Tragic Meeting

In October 1860, an incident took place at Apache Pass, a narrow crossing between two mountains in southeastern Arizona, which had grim results. A band of Apache raided a ranch that belonged to a white man named John Ward. They stole some cattle and kidnapped Felix Ward, the ranch owner's son. A small unit of soldiers looked for the boy but without success.

Several months later, in 1861, the army assigned Second Lieutenant George Bascom and a company of some fifty troops to conduct a more thorough search. Bascom invited Chief Cochise to come to a meeting at Apache Pass to discuss the matter. Cochise replied that he knew nothing of the incident, which was true. Nevertheless, he agreed to attend. Following tradition, he and a band of his subchiefs prepared for the meeting by having the women scrub them thoroughly, comb their hair, and paint their faces.

Cochise, 1815–1874

Cochise, a powerful chief of the Chiricahua Apache, was a dominant figure in Indian-white relations in the turbulent American southwest for nearly twenty-five years. Among Indian leaders, only Geronimo is better known today.

Like Mangas Coloradas, Cochise was tall with a muscular build. Cochise also married a daughter of Mangas Coloradas. The couple had two children, both boys, named Taza and Naiche.

During the years of violence between the Chiricahua and the white settlers and miners, Cochise and his followers used a rugged natural fortress in the Dragoon Mountains of Arizona as the base of operations. It came to serve as home for nearly a thousand of his followers, including about 250 warriors. From towering pinnacles of rock, Chiricahua sentinels watched for enemies. No white settlement beyond a hundred miles was safe from attack.

After Cochise's death, his son Taza succeeded him as chief. With Taza's sudden passing in 1876, Naiche became the leader of the Chiricahua. He and Geronimo were closely linked for several years until Geronimo's final surrender in 1886.

During the 1860s and 1870s, the mighty Cochise, pictured here in an oil painting, was the undisputed leader of the Chiricahua Apache.

At the meeting, held inside a big army tent, Bascom demanded that Cochise return the kidnapped boy. Cochise said he was innocent and even offered to help find the youngster. Bascom did not believe the chief.

Once the meeting was over, Bascom invited Cochise and other Indians to go into another tent where he said a fine dinner was awaiting them. Once the Indians were inside, soldiers surrounded the tent, then moved to seize the Indians and hold them as prisoners.

Army Second Lieutenant George Bascom helped to trigger a bitter encounter between the U.S. Army and Chiricahua chief Cochise and his people.

Cochise reacted quickly. He sprang to the side of the tent, whipped out his knife, slashed an opening in the tent wall, and escaped. But Bascom and his soldiers seized the other Indians and held them as prisoners. After that, relations between the whites and Indians slipped quickly downhill.

The Start of a Long Struggle

Cochise returned to his tribe to describe Bascom's treachery. Soon after, his warriors blockaded the wagon road through Apache Pass. They ambushed travelers and captured some of them. Then Cochise sent a message to Bascom offering to exchange his prisoners for the Apache he held. Bascom refused. Not long after, Cochise and his warriors discovered the captured Indians hanging from trees where they had been executed.

Cochise boiled with anger. The Indians cut down the bodies of their comrades and buried them. Then they killed the whites they had captured and hung them from the same trees. So ended a decade of peace between the whites and Indians.

Geronimo was not present at what the Apache came to call the "Cut Through the Tent" affair. At the time, Geronimo and other members of his Bedonkohe group were living among the Chiricahua. Geronimo had married again to a woman named She-gha, a close relative of Cochise's family. Sometime later, he took a second wife, Shtsha-she, a Bedonkohe woman. Throughout his life as a warrior, Geronimo often held to the practice of having two or even three wives at a time.

After Geronimo learned of the incident, he realized its great importance. ". . . All of the Indians agreed not to be friendly with the white men any more. There was no general engagement, but a long struggle followed."

To say it was merely a "long struggle" was to greatly minimize what took place. Cochise sent out scouts to watch every stagecoach line, wagon road, settler's home, and company of soldiers. The scouts reported any activity by whites to signalmen posted in the hills. A puff of smoke or, at night, small flickers from a campfire would convey a message.

Bands of warriors scattered throughout the area were awaiting such signals. When one came, the band would strike. Homes and ranch buildings were burned, cattle killed, and crops in the fields destroyed. The attack would last only a few minutes. Then the raiders would speed into the hills.

A Recognized Apache Leader

Geronimo was an eager participant in these attacks. Heading a band of forty or so warriors, he raced from ranch to ranch, burning and killing. Being one of the first Apache to learn of the line (called the international boundary line) that now separated the United States and Mexico, Geronimo used that knowledge to his advantage. Soldiers from one country were not permitted to cross the line and enter the territory of the other. Following a raid, Geronimo and his band would race from the United States across the line into Mexico. He knew that his pursuers could not follow.

Geronimo was also one of the first Apache to be aware that some units of the U.S. **Cavalry** were equipped with rifles that fired cartridges. These were the small metal containers that held the bullet, plus the powder that provided the explosive charge. Such weapons were far superior to the old powder-and-ball muskets that most Indians used. The new rifles could be reloaded quicker and were far more accurate. Geronimo made it a priority to ambush cavalrymen that carried such weapons. Before long, Geronimo's continued success in raiding and warring spread his fame throughout the

Fully aware of the existence of the international boundary line, Geronimo, after conducting attacks on whites in the American southwest, would flee across the border into Mexico—much like in this c. 1885 lithograph that pictures hostile Indians on the warpath.

Southwest. Frantic messages went out from the Department of the Army in Washington, D.C., to units in the field to capture or kill Geronimo at any cost. Among the Chiricahua who felt their culture being threatened by the whites, Geronimo was now regarded as the Apache who could best deal with the enemy. He grew in stature as a result. While not a chief in a traditional sense of the word, Geronimo came to be looked upon as a true leader.

CHAPTER 4

Murder and Vengeance

Men, that old murderer [Mangas Coloradas] has got away from every soldier command and has left a trail of blood for 5,000 miles on the old stage line. . . . I want him dead.

—Colonel John R. West

Since the "Cut Through the Tent" incident, the violent clashes between the Apache and the whites had worsened. Then, in early 1863, a party of gold prospectors crossed into Apache territory and camped at Fort McLane in southern New Mexico. Like other forts in the area, the army had abandoned Fort McLane after the Civil War had erupted in 1861, and federal troops were shifted from the Southwest to serve with battlefield units in the East.

The prospectors, fearful of being attacked by Apache, decided to kidnap Mangas Coloradas and hold him hostage. Only when they had safely completed their gold-hunting mission would they release the Indian chief.

Death of Mangas Coloradas

Several of the gold seekers set out on horseback to Pinos Altos, where they knew Mangas and his followers would be found. They were joined by an army unit under the command of Brigadier General James Henry Carleton, who was no friend of the Indians. In fact, he was quite the opposite. He had issued an order to those serving in his command "to kill all Indian men wherever found."

As the group of prospectors and soldiers neared the settlement at Pinos Altos, they raised a white flag of truce and waited. Soon Mangas Coloradas and several of his subchiefs came forward. Without any warning, the soldiers suddenly pulled out their rifles and trained them on the chief. He was then quickly taken prisoner and brought to Fort McLane. The startled Apache were told that Mangas would be safe as long no harm befell the prospectors.

That night at Fort McLane, two soldiers guarded Mangas. Since it was bitterly cold, they kept a fire burning. During the night, one of the prospectors saw the soldiers heat their metal bayonets in the fire and then press them against Mangas's legs and feet as he slept. Mangas awakened to the searing pain and shouted angrily. Still raging, he raised himself to one elbow. When he did, the guards blasted him with rifle fire. To complete the execution, they drew their revolvers and emptied them into his bleeding and lifeless body.

Since the "Cut Through the Tent" incident, the violent clashes between the Apache and the whites had worsened.

Later, the army issued an untruthful report on the killing of Mangas. According to the report, Mangas had tried to escape three times. On the third attempt, the guards shot him. But a prospector who had witnessed what had taken place gave an entirely different version. He stated that Colonel John R. West, the officer in charge of the guards, told them, "Men, that old murderer [Mangas Coloradas] has got away from every soldier command and has left a trail of blood for 5,000 miles on the old stage line. I want him

The Name Debate

In January 1863, after the seizure and fatal shooting of Mangas Coloradas, Geronimo called his murder the "greatest wrong ever done to the Indians." In using the word *Indians*, Geronimo was referring to all humans that shared his tribal origins.

The word *Indians* was common in Geronimo's time. Its use went back to Christopher Columbus. In making landfall in the Caribbean at the end of the fifteenth century, Columbus mistakenly believed that he had reached the Indies and started calling the people he encountered "Indians." For centuries, the native people of North and South America were referred to by that name.

A hand-colored print from the mid–19th century depicts Christopher Columbus trading with the local natives he met. He called them "Indians" because he thought he had reached the Indies.

Beginning in the 1960s, an effort was made to scrap the word *Indian* in favor of *Native American* when describing the natives of the **contiguous** United States. It was thought to be the more accurate term, and the term *Native American* came into general use.

Today, there is a general preference for *Indian* or, more properly, *American Indian*. But *Native American* is often used as well.

dead or alive tomorrow morning, do you understand, I want him dead." The message to the guards was clear.

Geronimo was shocked when he learned of Mangas's death and how he had been killed. The Apache leader now feared that the same troops who had captured and killed Mangas would attack his band. He told his people they must leave immediately for a mountain hideaway not far from Apache Pass. Once on their journey, they came upon four white men and a herd of cattle. "We killed all four," Geronimo recalled. "We drove the cattle back into the mountains, made a camp, and began to kill the cattle and pack the meat."

Apache Vengeance

That was only the beginning. The Apache took their revenge for the murder of Mangas Coloradas by unleashing a long reign of terror. Cochise struck often, attacking what army posts remained in central Arizona. He also targeted white settlers. From hideaways in the mountains of Mexico, Geronimo terrorized much of southern Arizona. Juh, head of the Nednai Apache and Geronimo's close friend, also led his raiders north out of Mexico to burn and plunder the ever-widening white settlements.

The white people of Arizona were unable to cope with the fierceness of the Indian raids. They cried out

Following the death of Mangas Coloradas, the Apache sought revenge by attacking white settlers. This illustration from an issue of *Harper's Monthly* in 1891 shows an Indian, perhaps an Apache, aiming a rifle toward a covered wagon.

to the federal government for help, saying that the "bloodthirsty savages" were running wild. But the government, represented by the U.S. Army, could do little.

The settlers were angry and frustrated. Their mood would soon turn to rage and violence—as it did in the predawn hours of April 30, 1871, at Camp Grant in Arizona.

Incident at Camp Grant

Located on the San Pedro River about fifty miles northeast of what is now Tucson, Arizona, Camp Grant consisted of a forlorn collection of sun-baked **adobe** buildings. Lieutenant Royal E. Whitman was serving as the post commander. Unlike many of the unsympathetic military officers, Lieutenant Whitman had turned Camp Grant into a place of safety for formerly hostile Apache. He put some of them to work as farmworkers, and a few ranchers

Camp Grant, pictured in this early 1870s photograph, was a place of refuge for the Apache.

even hired some of those Apache who now made their home at Camp Grant.

As a group, the Camp Grant Apache were content and cooperative, glad that their days as warriors had ended. They even sent runners to other Apache groups urging them to surrender. The people of Tucson at first praised Lieutenant Whitman for what he had done. But as Apache raids and killings continued in the area, Tucson citizens began to suspect the raiders were from Camp Grant.

Early in April, there was more violence involving another Indian tribe. An Apache raiding party, unprovoked, attacked a settlement of Papago Indians at San Xavier del Bac and drove off their cattle and horses. The Papago were a peaceful Indian tribe, whose members farmed and hunted. To most settlers, they were the "best" Indians in Arizona.

A few days later, **renegade** Apache struck a white village at San Pedro. One settler was killed.

Many Tucson people now believed the time had come to take action. Their newspaper, the *Arizona Citizen*, gave them support. There was, said the newspaper, "no reasonable doubt that the Camp Grant–fed Indians

After an Apache raiding party attacked a settlement of the peaceful Papago Indians (two of whom are pictured here in a c. 1855 print), some members of the tribe turned vengeful and joined in the attack on Camp Grant.

Army lieutenant Royal E. Whitman, shown here in a photograph from the 1860s, was post commander at Camp Grant and played a key role in Apache affairs during the early 1870s.

made the raid on San Xavier . . . and in stronger force . . . attacked the San Pedro settlement." Lieutenant Whitman was quick to deny that any Camp Grant Indians were involved in the attacks. But few settlers listened to him.

The Tucson citizens held a meeting and formed a war party to attack Camp Grant. They enlisted the support of the Papago. Almost one hundred members of the tribe volunteered to join the attacking force. Early on the morning April 30, 1871, the war party set out for Camp Grant. When they arrived, they found that most of the Apache men were on a hunting expedition in the north. The Papago rushed the settlement with heavy clubs and knives. They moved furtively among the wickiups, killing Apache women and children. Settlers with rifles picked off those who tried to escape. The slaughter was over in less than an hour. About one hundred Apache were murdered.

In Washington, President Ulysses S. Grant branded the Camp Grant attack as "murder." He demanded that those who took part in the attack should stand trial. A grand jury met in Tucson later in 1871 and charged 108 men, both settlers and Papago, with murder. As the trial unfolded, those accused were calm. They were fully aware that the local citizens believed that their terrible crime had been justified.

The defense attorney made no effort to hide the fact that a massacre had taken place. Instead, he argued that the attack was warranted because of the relentless Apache raiding and killing, which he linked to the Indians at Camp Grant. It took only nineteen minutes for the jury to decide the issue. The verdict: not guilty.

A Move for Peace

Not long after the trial, President Grant decided to send General Oliver O. Howard to Arizona to see whether he could bring peace to the area. President Grant had what he believed was a solution to the problem. The federal government would move the Apache and other Indian tribes from their ancestral homelands and relocate them on parcels of land, called reservations, that had been set aside for them. The president hoped that General Howard would be able to meet with Cochise and his tribal leaders, including Geronimo, to bring this about.

General Howard was a good choice. Known as the "praying general," he had a reputation for fairness in dealing with the Indians in the past. His latest assignment would severely test his better qualities.

CHAPTER 5

An Apache Reservation?

[General Howard] always kept his word with us and treated us as brothers. We never had so good a friend among the United States officers as General Howard.

General Howard knew that none of his plans for peace, which included the removal of the Apache to reservation lands, could succeed unless they had the support of Cochise. In 1872, in an effort to arrange a meeting with the Indian chief, General Howard paid a visit to the Tularosa Agency, a government office that managed matters dealing with the Indians, in western New Mexico. While he was there, a cavalry troop arrived. The troop guide was Tom Jeffords.

General Howard couldn't believe his good luck. Tom Jeffords, a trusted friend of Cochise, had been the supervisor of a mail line that became part of the famous **pony express** system. Some of his mail riders had been ambushed and killed by Apache raiders. Furious, Jeffords rode by himself into Cochise's camp to seek a meeting with the chief. Cochise was so impressed with Jeffords's bravery that he promised him safe passage for his riders in the future. The two men became trusted friends. General Howard realized that Jeffords could be the key to the success of his mission for peace.

Tom Jeffords's close friendship with Cochise enabled him to aid General Oliver O. Howard in negotiating a peace agreement with the Apache chief.

The general asked Jeffords whether he had actually visited Cochise's stronghold in the Dragoon Mountains. When Jeffords replied that he had, General Howard asked Jeffords to take him there.

Jeffords thought for a moment, and then said, "Yes, General Howard, I will; but you must go without any soldiers." General Howard agreed to do so, taking only his aide and three other men rather than a whole troop of soldiers.

Jeffords asked Chee, Cochise's nephew, to join their group. Jeffords knew that Chee was a man that Cochise fully trusted. Ponce, whose father was a close friend of Cochise, also agreed to go along. Ponce spoke Spanish. He would be useful as an interpreter. Jeffords also asked a handful of other Indians to accompany the group.

Into the Mountains

When the group reached the trail that would lead to Cochise's land, Chee sent up a smoke signal and barked like a coyote. Immediately, a reply came from nearby. They had come upon one of Cochise's outposts. About sixty Chiricahua men, women, and children were camped at the site.

One of Cochise's scouts told Howard that he must reduce the size of his group. The general did so by instructing three men to leave and wait for him at Fort Bowie. The party now included just five men—General Howard, Jeffords, Chee, Ponce, and Captain Sladon, who was an aide to the general.

After leaving the outpost, the five men still had about one hundred miles to travel. They crossed the Chiricahua Mountains, passed through San Simon Valley, and entered the foothills of the Dragoon Mountains. They stopped several times to enable Chee and Ponce time to build five fires in a circle—an Apache signal that indicated five men were approaching in peace.

Eventually, they came to a wide canyon with towering walls that shielded acres of good grass and several springs. They camped there for the night.

The next day, Cochise rode in. With him were his wife, his sister, and his teenage son Naiche. Howard could not help but be impressed by the Indian chief. He stood a head above his fellow Apache. He had large dark eyes and a pleasant look. His black hair was touched with strands of silver.

The chief greeted Jeffords warmly and then shook hands with General Howard. "Buenos dias," Cochise said.

The two groups sat in a semicircle. General Howard explained that he had come to make peace between the chief and the white people.

"Nobody wants peace more than I do," said Cochise.

A General's Promise

Cochise was now a man in his seventies. He knew that there was no warrior who was clever or powerful enough to lead the Chiricahua after his death. He had two sons, but both were young, still in their teens.

He was determined to make an agreement with General Howard that would assure a peaceful future for the Chiricahua.

He was determined to make an agreement with General Howard that would assure a peaceful future for the Chiricahua.

General Howard began by suggesting a possible site for the Chiricahua's reservation. It was along the Rio Grande, where there was good grazing for cattle. A frown crossed Cochise's face. He had little enthusiasm for the site. The chief offered a suggestion of his own. "Why not give me Apache Pass?" he said. "Give me that and I will protect all the roads. I will see that nobody's property is taken by Indians."

Cochise then had another request. He wanted his tribal leaders to join the conference. They lived deep in the mountains. It would take about ten days for them to arrive. The general agreed to wait. Geronimo was one of Cochise's tribal leaders who arrived for the conference. Geronimo liked General Howard from the beginning and would later look upon him with affection and gratitude.

Once the discussions began again, General Howard agreed to give Cochise and the Chiricahua, including the Bedonkohe,

Major General Oliver O. Howard, in a photograph from the 1860s, was Geronimo's trusted friend.

exactly what the chief had asked for. They were to be granted their entire Apache Pass homeland as their reservation—and it was to be theirs forever. A government order later confirmed the arrangement. The southern boundary line of the reservation was to be the Mexican border. It extended fifty-six miles west of the Arizona–New Mexico line and included the Chiricahua and Dragoon mountains and the Sulphur Springs Valley in between.

Cochise asked that Tom Jeffords be made the reservation agent. General Howard consented to that, too. As the agent of the reservation, Jeffords would be in charge of all reservation operations. He would place orders with the federal government for the food, clothing, and blankets needed by the Chiricahua.

Reservations and Removal

The idea of the federal government removing tribes of Indians and assigning them to live on tracts of public land called reservations was not new. It dates to the nation's earliest days. As early as 1786, with the white population growing, the idea of restricting the Indians to certain areas began to take shape.

Actual removal of the Indians from their homelands came later. Although it was supposed to be voluntary, removal was sometimes backed by force, and with tragic results. Under President Andrew Jackson, Congress passed the Indian Removal Act of 1830. This gave the president the power to exchange Indian land east of the Mississippi River for land west of the river.

When General Ulysses S. Grant became president in 1869, he pursued a "peace policy" with the Indians. It called for tribes to be relocated from their traditional lands to reservations that would be created for them. But the program was not successful. The Indians often lived under pitiable conditions, and the system was plagued by fraud and corruption on the part of those who managed it.

With changes, the reservation system lived on. Today, there are slightly more than three hundred Indian reservations in the United States. Some are huge. About twenty-five reservations are bigger than the state of Rhode Island.

This painting by Robert Lindneux depicts the Trail of Tears, the name given to the forced and tragic journey of the Cherokee Indians to Indian Territory (now the state of Oklahoma) during the 1830s.

Above is a modern photograph of Apache Pass, a vital route between two mountain ranges in southeastern Arizona where Apache and whites often came into conflict.

General Howard, however, wondered whether Geronimo could really be happy living in a world with no violence. "I believe," said Howard, "he was not yet quite sure that it was time for peace to come."

General Howard was right in his judgment. Geronimo had his doubts about the agreement. Like many other Apache, he remembered how Cochise had been the victim of a breach of faith on the part of Second Lieutenant Bascom at Apache Pass. And there was not an Apache who would ever forget or forgive the murder of Mangas Coloradas. Geronimo could not help but harbor a feeling of distrust. The future was to provide justification for his lack of faith.

CHAPTER 6

Broken Promise

We are not going to San Carlos with you, and unless you are very careful, you and your Apache police will not go back to San Carlos either.

With the Chiricahua now living in peace on the vast Apache Pass reservation, Cochise and Tom Jeffords worked together to maintain order and harmony. And since Apache Pass was already the Chiricahua homeland, the tribe did not have to move.

Jeffords permitted the Chiricahua to keep their rifles and horses, and he allowed the tribe plenty of freedom of movement. He got the medicines the Chiricahua needed, even though he sometimes had to pay for them out of his own pocket. The tribesmen and their families were thus able to escape some of the illnesses that swept other reservations.

Cochise did his part, too. When cattle that had been stolen by Apache raiders turned up on the reservation, the Chiricahua leader ordered them to be turned over to Jeffords.

Outlaw and Raider

Geronimo, however, was a problem. He had no desire to become a farmer and live on the reservation. Instead, he continued his career as a raider. From within the Apache Pass reservation, where he had settled with his family, Geronimo and his raiding parties struck deep into Mexico. Mexican cavalry units could do little to stop them. If they

picked up the outlaws' trails and pursued them, Geronimo would race for the border. Once on the other side, he knew he would be safe because Mexican troops were not permitted to cross into the United States.

To the reservation families, the U.S. Indian Bureau issued allowances of food on a regular basis, usually every ten days. This was a direct benefit to Geronimo. He did not have to worry about providing for his family. The federal government was seeing to it that they were fed and clothed. Geronimo could devote himself to raiding Mexican settlements on a full-time basis.

Geronimo, however, was a problem. He had no desire to . . . live on the reservation. Instead, he continued his career as a raider.

Tom Jeffords knew about the raids. But as the agent of the reservation, he had some two thousand Apache to care for. He could not control them all, and Mexico was not part of his concern. Cochise was aware of the attacks, too. While he did not approve of them, he did nothing to bring them to an end. He had made a peace treaty with the United States, he felt, not with Mexico.

Death of Cochise

The renowned and respected Cochise died in June 1874, but the Chiricahua kept the circumstances a secret. The tribe did not reveal his burial place, either. With the passing of Cochise, Apache-white relations headed steadily downhill.

Before he died, Cochise made Taza and his younger brother, Naiche, promise that they would preserve the peace agreement he had entered into with General Howard. But both sons lacked their father's ability as a leader.

A print from the late 1880s shows an Apache raiding party attacking and burning a white settler's home and assaulting members of the family.

In April 1876, Apache-white relations suddenly turned violent. Although Geronimo was not directly responsible, a stagecoach was attacked and the station keeper, his assistant, and some other white men were killed. In quick succession, settlers' houses were burned and cattle stolen. Fear and terror tormented the whites of southern Arizona.

Wrongful Act

Meanwhile in Washington, the federal government was putting the finishing touches on a change of policy that was to deeply affect the lives of every Apache. "Consolidation," it was called. Under its terms, all of the Apache tribes of Arizona and southwestern New Mexico were to be brought together on one reservation—the San Carlos Reservation in southern Arizona.

The fact that General Howard had granted Apache Pass to the Chiricahua "forever" was ignored. It was as if the agreement between them had never been made. By government order, the Chiricahua were to be uprooted and moved.

The federal government claimed that it would have greater control over the Apache by putting them all in one place. They would thus be able to prevent raids into Mexico. But this argument carried little weight. By shifting the Chiricahua to the San Carlos Reservation, they were actually moving them closer to Mexico. This undoubtedly meant that there would be more raiding in Mexico, not less.

Moving the Apache Reservation

Early in May 1876, the commissioner of Indian Affairs in Washington gave the order for the removal of the Chiricahua from Apache Pass. Tom Jeffords was dismissed as the reservation's agent. John Clum, the new agent for the San Carlos Reservation was handed the difficult task of removing the Chiricahua from their Apache Pass home and settling them at San Carlos. With this role, Clum came to be known as the "White Chief of the Apaches."

Supported by a unit of federal troops, Clum arrived at Apache Pass in June 1876 to find the Chiricahua in a state of chaos. A group of them had gotten drunk and gone on a violent spree. They killed several whites and stole their horses. When the rampaging band sought to seize control of the Chiricahua tribe, Taza and Naiche killed one of the group's leaders and wounded another.

The violence against the whites aroused the settlers, who wanted the government to retaliate. The *Arizona Citizen*, a newspaper with a white readership, had a bloodthirsty solution.

John Clum (center), who took command of the troubled San Carlos Reservation, poses with two Native Americans at the reservation in 1875.

The newspaper called for a "steady unrelenting, hopeless . . . war" against the Apache, "slaying men, women, and children."

Arizona governor Anson Safford was more reasonable. He asked only that the federal government shift all Indians from Apache Pass at once. That is exactly what John Clum had decided to do. In a meeting with Taza and Naiche, Clum announced that the removal of the tribe was to begin the next morning. Taza and Naiche had no objection, and Geronimo was expected to move as well. Before the meeting ended, a young boy came into the camp to tell Clum that Geronimo wanted to see him.

Naiche, shown here with his wife in a c. 1884 photograph, was the son of Cochise.

Clum had blamed Geronimo for many of the Apache's troubles—and rightly so. He looked upon Geronimo as a completely lawless person, deceitful and untrustworthy. Even so, Clum agreed to meet with him. But Clum was taking no chances. He prepared for the conference by posting armed guards with loaded rifles about the site.

The added security hardly seemed necessary. When Geronimo walked into camp, his usual scowl was gone, replaced by a thin-lipped smile. He greeted Clum warmly, although he seemed tense. He said he had become alarmed following the recent violence. He then declared that he and his people wanted peace. They were ready to go with the others to San Carlos. Clum breathed a sigh of relief.

But there was a problem, Geronimo explained. His people could not go the next day. They were camped about twenty miles away. It would take him about three days to travel to their campsite and lead them back. Would Clum wait the three days? Clum really had no choice. He had to consent.

Geronimo, as he appeared late in life, assumed his thin-lipped smile for this portrait painted by E. A. Burbank.

Three days passed. Geronimo and his people did not appear. Clum asked a few scouts to find the camp and tell Geronimo to hurry along. The scouts quickly located the camp. It was only three miles away, not twenty. But it was abandoned. Only the slightest traces of Geronimo and his followers remained. Geronimo had fled, probably to Mexico. Wherever he was headed, he had a three-day start.

The next time the two men met, Clum vowed, the outcome would be different.

Mountain Hideout

After making his getaway, Geronimo led his followers into the difficult and dangerous terrain of Mexico's Sierra Madre. They scrambled up the soaring mountain ridges that sometimes reached heights of ten thousand feet. From their vantage point, they could keep an eye on their pursuers. If they were unable to halt those giving chase, they would ascend farther up the ridge. If the troops did manage to get close, the Indians would scatter like a flight of sparrows.

From his mountain headquarters, Geronimo led his warriors on one raid after another into Arizona, making off with hundreds of horses and cattle, which they hid in the mountains. They also looted, burned, and killed white settlers.

The army assigned fresh cavalry units to Arizona with orders to halt the raiding and to capture Geronimo. But the cavalry was

A recent photograph of Mexico's Sierra Madre shows the rugged terrain where Geronimo and his followers carved out their hideaways.

In an illustration that dates to 1886, Geronimo (far right) poses with three of his warriors (left to right), Yahnozha, Chappo, and Fun.

no match for the elusive Geronimo and his warriors. He posted scouts with powerful binoculars to keep watch from mountain lookouts. Their smoke signals kept Geronimo aware of the cavalry's movements.

Sometimes Geronimo and his band would ambush a cavalry unit. They would strike fast, kill a handful of soldiers, and then dash back across the border to their mountain hideout. In almost a year of raiding Arizona ranches, no warrior in Geronimo's band was killed or captured.

Return of an Outlaw

Late in 1876, Geronimo abruptly halted his attacks. He decided he had accumulated as much livestock as he could care for, and that it was time for him to sell his stolen herds. He found the ranchers in New Mexico and the Mexican towns along the Rio Grande to be eager buyers.

By mid-March 1877, Geronimo had sold most of his cattle and horses. He and his followers then set out for the Warm Springs Reservation in the southwestern corner of New Mexico. He was not being pursued there and felt he could get food and clothing for his family and others in his band.

There on the reservation, an army officer happened to spot him. He reported that Geronimo and his followers were tending a herd of about one hundred horses. While living on the reservation, the brash Apache also had the nerve to complain that the agency was not issuing him the rations of food and clothing he wanted. Also, by this time, Geronimo had been branded a renegade by the federal government. That he would have the audacity to request food rations was the last straw. The government felt forced to act. On March 20, 1877, the commissioner of Indian Affairs issued orders to John Clum. "[Take] your Indian police and arrest renegade Indians at Ojo Caliente [Warm Springs], New Mexico. . . . Remove renegades to San Carlos and hold them in confinement for murder and robbery."

Clum was in his headquarters at the San Carlos Reservation when he received the message. Warm Springs was some four hundred miles to the east. Barren desert and rugged mountains made up the terrain between the two reservations. But Clum had been waiting for the chance to meet with Geronimo again. He gathered together about one hundred Indian peace officers from the reservation and set out. Companies of the U.S. Calvary would meet him at Warm Springs, he was told.

> *Also, by this time, Geronimo had been branded a renegade by the federal government.*

Deadly Face-off

Weeks later, when Clum drew near the Warm Springs agency, he sent a message to Geronimo and other tribal leaders requesting a meeting. The reason for the meeting was not stated, but the messengers seemed friendly, so Geronimo agreed to meet with Clum.

Clum was waiting on the porch of the agency building with half a dozen police officers when Geronimo arrived. A group of about fifty armed warriors were with him. They dismounted and stood silently. Clum spoke. In a commanding voice, he accused Geronimo and his band of killing ranchers and stealing horses and cattle. He declared that they had broken the peace treaty between Cochise and General Howard. It did not matter that it had been the U.S. government that had broken the treaty by forcing the Apache tribes

A modern painting by John Walker depicts a defiant Geronimo at the Warm Springs Reservation, where the Apache leader's confrontation with John Clum led to his capture.

to move from their Apache Pass reservation. Then Clum announced that he was taking Geronimo and his warriors back to the San Carlos Reservation.

Geronimo answered boldly. "We are not going to San Carlos with you, and unless you are very careful, you and your Apache police will not go back to San Carlos either. Your bodies will stay here at Ojo Caliente [Warm Springs] to make food for coyotes."

Clum was not surprised by Geronimo's resistance. He was prepared for the Apache's defiance and had earlier posted agents armed with rifles in nearby reservation buildings. When Clum raised his left hand and touched the brim of his hat, dozens of police officers burst forth. They gathered about Geronimo and his followers.

Keeping his eyes trained on Geronimo, Clum saw the cunning Apache's thumb move toward the hammer of his .50 caliber Springfield rifle. In another instant, Geronimo could explode a bullet to the target of his choice. But the agent was ready with another signal. He touched the butt of his own Colt .45. His officers raised their rifles and aimed them at Geronimo and the others. Clum saw Geronimo draw his thumb back. He saw the warrior's shoulders slump. Clum knew he had won.

He announced to Geronimo and the others that they were prisoners. Then they were marched to the reservation blacksmith shop. There, iron chains were put on their wrists and ankles. Geronimo, now nearing his fiftieth year, seemed willing to accept his defeat. "It is well," he said. "We have been on the warpath a long time and are tired. If you want to have a big smoke and big talk we are ready."

Clum saw no reason to talk. Within a few days, Geronimo and his followers were loaded into wagons to be carried off under military guard to San Carlos. Clum's seizure of Geronimo marked the first time in his life that the Apache warrior had been captured. It would never happen again.

CHAPTER 7

Breakout

Officers and soldiers serving in this department are reminded that one of the fundamental principles of the military character is justice to all—Indians as well as white men.

—General George Crook

Once Geronimo and his followers arrived at the San Carlos Reservation, they were locked into the guardhouse. Clum planned to bring Geronimo into a court of law and have him tried for the vast amount of bloodshed he had caused. According to Clum, Geronimo had murdered at least one hundred men, women, and children, and the agent wanted to see Geronimo hanged for his crimes.

For all that he had achieved for the federal government, Clum wanted to be rewarded. He sent a message to the commissioner of Indian Affairs in Washington, D.C., saying that he would like to be given an increase in his salary. He also asked for the funds to hire and train more Indians to be police officers. Both of Clum's requests were quickly turned down.

Clum was livid. He immediately resigned his post as agent for the San Carlos Reservation.

A New Way of Life

Clum's resignation may have preserved Geronimo's life. Soon after the angry agent's departure, a new reservation agent was named. The idea of prosecuting Geronimo for his assorted crimes was conveniently forgotten.

The new agent, not wishing to trigger unrest among Geronimo's followers, set the Apache renegade free. But his freedom had limits. Geronimo was made to understand his days as a raider were over. He was to become a "good Indian." He was to remain within the reservation borders and go to work farming. Geronimo agreed to live peaceably.

Most of the many hundreds of other Apache on the San Carlos Reservation had also submitted to this new way of life, so that they, too, could live in peace. They realized that Geronimo's raiding, killing, and cattle stealing were the cause of many of their problems. But there were some Apache at San Carlos who were wholly frustrated with reservation life. They felt that they were being cheated by the agents in the amounts of food and clothing

In a photograph dating to 1886, heavily guarded Apache prisoners at the San Carlos Reservation work hard digging an irrigation channel—an important element in the federal government's plan to make farmers out of the tribespeople.

they were being given. They wanted to return to their old ways. When Geronimo unfolded a plan for escaping from the reservation, they listened.

Apache prisoners at the San Carlos Reservation form long lines to receive food allotments on what was called "Ration and Beef Day."

In September 1881, Geronimo made his move, leading a break from San Carlos. He and his followers headed across the border and toward the Sierra Madre. They killed every person they happened to meet and stole supplies and horses as they fled. Both the army and a civilian posse set out after them, but the fleeing Apache made good their escape.

But Geronimo soon found that life as a renegade was now much more difficult than what it had been before. The United States had entered into a treaty with Mexico that allowed the soldiers of either nation to cross the international boundary at will when pursuing **marauding** Indians. No longer would the border serve as a solid wall, halting the passage of troops to the north or south.

A New Commander

In 1882, the United States also acted by assigning General George Crook to take full command in Arizona. The army's most skilled and effective Indian fighter, Crook had had dealings with the Apache at an earlier time. In 1871, after General Crook had taken command in Arizona, he sought to bring peace to the Arizona Territory in keeping with President Grant's wishes. Crook

General George Crook, pictured in a photograph from the 1870s, was both fair-minded and shrewd in dealing with the Apache.

remained there until 1875. By the time he left, he had greatly strengthened the military and had also provided for the humane treatment of the Apache and other Indians.

When he returned to Arizona, Crook saw only disorder and criminal behavior. The Apache complained to General Crook about dishonest reservation agents who would steal the food and clothing that had been provided for the Indians by the government. The agents would then sell these items to traders in the nearby town of Globe.

Hunger was another frequent complaint. Twenty people were expected to live for a week on wretched cuts of beef and only twenty cups of flour. When a family needed buckskin with which to make moccasins, they had to buy it from the agent. Interpreters, whom the government made available to enable the

THE REASON OF THE INDIAN OUTBREAK.
General Miles declares that the Indians are starved into rebellion.

A cartoon from the magazine *Judge* in December 1890 supports the belief that reservation uprisings and breakouts were caused by crooked government agents who grew rich by privately selling food allotments meant for the Apache, who ended up starving.

Apache to communicate with the agents, also demanded that the Indians pay for their services.

Adding to the Indians' misery was the discovery of coal, copper, and other mineral resources on land on which the Apache lived. The reservation had been reduced in size five times so mines could be put into private hands. With each reduction, families were uprooted and forced to find new home sites on the ever-shrinking reservation.

By the time General Crook arrived, there were less than a thousand Apache living on the San Carlos Reservation. They were mostly very young or very old. Most of the able-bodied males, wholly dissatisfied with reservation life, had fled like Geronimo. Also like Geronimo, many had joined outlaw bands in Mexico. From their mountain camps, they raided white settlements almost without letup.

Making Changes

General Crook moved decisively to put an end to all such abuses. Once his survey of conditions was completed, he issued a report of his findings. In it, the general said that he found "a general feeling of distrust and want of confidence in the whites, especially in the soldiery." He reminded the officers and soldiers "that one of the fundamental principles of the military character is justice to all—Indians as well as white men."

Crook also sent messages to the bands of Apache who had left the reservation. Those who returned would not be imprisoned or otherwise punished. He promised that the federal government would protect them. They would be fed and clothed. Those who did not return would be tracked down and punished.

Also, like Geronimo, many had joined outlaw bands in Mexico.

Crook's fair-minded policy of dealing with the Indians soon brought results. Large groups of Apache began returning to San Carlos. Raiding lessened.

Crook also noted that there were many people living on the reservation who did not belong there. These included miners, prospectors, and assorted fortune seekers. Crook ordered his soldiers to escort all such people to the reservation borders.

Once Crook felt that reservation was operating in a proper manner, he turned his attention to Geronimo's outlaw band. Early in March 1883, as Crook was planning a strategy for capturing Geronimo, a group of Chiricahua from deep in the Sierra Madre

Brutal and treacherous as an Apache warrior and raider, Chatto later became a loyal scout for General Crook.

raided several Arizona ranches. Led by a fearless young chief named Chatto, they were guilty of terrible acts of brutality.

Pointing the Way

For Crook, this was an opportunity he had been waiting for. He would follow the trail left by Chatto's band. He felt certain it would lead not only to Chatto's mountain stronghold but also to the hideout of Geronimo and his followers.

To help track down Geronimo, Crook planned to use his own troops as well as Apache scouts, whom he recruited from the reservation. These scouts were tall, strong warriors who were shrewd and had great endurance. They were skilled in tracking as well as making their way through the woods and mountains. They were also, of course, knowledgeable in the ways of the Apache.

Crook assembled a force of nearly two hundred Apache scouts. They told him that they were eager to help bring peace to the Apache so that eventually they could all live and work together with the whites. Several army officers and a company of about fifty mounted troops joined the scouts. When the scouts were brought orders that they were to track Chatto's band into the Sierra Madre, they held a war dance to build up enthusiasm for the mission. The dance lasted all night. Traveling in groups of twos or threes, they set out the next morning. Their faces were painted a reddish color and they wore scarlet headbands to distinguish them from other Indians.

To help track down Geronimo, Crook planned to use his own troops as well as Apache scouts, whom he recruited from the reservation.

The scouts traveled on foot—some without any covering for their feet. Barefoot or wearing moccasins, they could cover thirty-five to forty miles a day. They were sharp-eyed and alert, able to identify every track in the sand or impression in the grass. They could even tell when a track had been made.

The scouts followed the trail left by the horses and cattle that Chatto's band had stolen. It led into the mountain ranges. Crook's soldiers struggled with the rough terrain. The heavily packed

An engraving from 1886 depicts Frederic Remington's rendering of a barefooted band of General Crook's Apache scouts as they seek to follow the trail leading to Geronimo.

mules stumbled and fell. But the Apache scouts moved with ease up and down the steep ridges.

When the advance party of scouts came upon what they believed to be Geronimo's base camp, they destroyed it after several hours of fierce fighting. Nine Apache were killed. Only a handful of captives were taken, including five children—three girls and two boys. The elusive Geronimo had fled and was nowhere to be found. But when Crook, who was trailing behind the advance scouting party, learned what had taken place, he set up a camp of his own. Apache began arriving to surrender. From them, Crook learned that Geronimo and a handful of his people were nearby and might attack. Crook's scouts piled up rocks and pine logs for defense. They would be ready.

CHAPTER 8

Surrender and Peace

Men, our people whom we left at our base camp are now in the hands of U.S. troops. What shall we do?

Geronimo was aware that his base camp had been taken over by soldiers from San Carlos. From his hiding place high in the mountains, he peered down at the camp. He could see the soldiers' tents and smoke from their campfires.

That the camp was occupied had come as no surprise to Geronimo and his followers. Days before, Geronimo, who was believed to have the powers of a prophet, and thus able to foretell the future, had predicted that such an event was going to take place.

Seeing into the Future

Geronimo had made his prediction as he and several of his men were returning to their camp after a long trek. One evening, when they were about one hundred miles from their camp and were feasting on a steer they had slaughtered, Geronimo said prophetically, "Men, our people whom we left at our base camp are now in the hands of U.S. troops. What shall we do?" Jason Betzinez, Geronimo's cousin, witnessed Geronimo give his startling prediction. "I cannot explain it to this day," Betzinez later reported, "But I was there and saw it. No, he didn't get the word by some messenger. And no smoke signals had been made."

This is a studio photograph of Jason Betzinez, Geronimo's cousin and lifelong friend, who was closely associated with him both as a warrior and, later, as a prisoner of war.

His people had faith in Geronimo and his powers. They believed what he had said. They started out immediately for their base camp. When they were not far from the campsite, Geronimo had another prediction to make. He said, "Tomorrow afternoon as we march along the north side of the mountains we will see a man standing on a hill to our left. He will howl to us and tell us that the troops have captured our base camp."

The next morning, they set out early. They made their way west through a forest of oaks and pines. That afternoon, they heard a man cry out to them from a hilltop off to their left. They recognized him as an Apache. The men, recalling what Geronimo had predicted, could hardly believe their eyes as the Indian made his way down the rock-strewn hill. When he reached the band, he reported that Geronimo's main camp was now in the hands of U.S. soldiers. Another **prophecy** by Geronimo had come true.

To find out what was going on at the camp, Geronimo sent two warriors down the mountain to investigate. Some time later, the two warriors climbed halfway back up the mountain. They shouted that General Crook was in charge of the troops and wanted to meet with Geronimo and his followers. While Geronimo was deciding what to do, some of the women and children in his band began to drift down the mountain and into the camp. To Crook's soldiers, they looked half-starved. The soldiers fed them army rations.

Coming to Terms

Geronimo and his followers were in desperate shape—starving and weary. They knew they had no choice but to give up. So the Apache leader and some of his men filed down to General Crook's camp. They moved cautiously, suspecting a trap.

Late in May 1883, when Geronimo finally met General Crook, the Apache leader declared that he and his followers were laying down their arms. But Geronimo had several demands. He told Crook that he and his followers were not to be punished for any crimes of the past. Once he and his band got back to San Carlos, they were to be given blankets and clothing. And once they had settled on the reservation, they must be supplied regularly with adequate food.

Geromino met General Crook in May 1883. A photograph from March 1886 depicts a second meeting between General George Crook and Geronimo.

Meanwhile, more and more members of Geronimo's band were coming out of the mountains to give up and were crowding into Crook's camp. Soldiers counted more than two hundred men and women who had already arrived. Stragglers appeared every day. Crook's food supplies were running low as a result.

Once Crook had agreed to Geronimo's demands, the Apache leader said he would return to San Carlos and take up farming again—but not right away. He said that he needed time to gather his widely scattered family members and their livestock. He promised to be at the border with his followers in "two moons," or two months. As it turned out, Geronimo did not mean two months, but a much longer, indefinite, span of time.

General Crook did not like the idea of waiting some unknown amount of time for Geronimo's return. But the general was in a difficult position. He was now burdened with an ever-increasing number of Apache. Day by day, his supplies were dwindling as he sought to keep them fed. He had to return to San Carlos with the Apache who had surrendered. Crook's only choice was to accept Geronimo's promise to return.

Of course, Crook's soldiers could have easily seized Geronimo, made him a prisoner, and taken him back to San Carlos in irons. But Crook felt it would be wrong to do such a thing. After all, Geronimo had given himself up without a struggle. To now make him a captive would have been a betrayal of trust.

A Grant of Independence

Geronimo surely realized he had gained the upper hand in his dealings with the general. Crook had tracked him down. He had gotten Geronimo to give himself up. But Geronimo was no prisoner. He was free to go wherever he pleased. A self-satisfied smile must have crossed his face as he watched Crook and his soldiers take down their tents, pack their belongings, mount their horses, and head north for San Carlos. More than three hundred Apache went with them.

Geronimo surely realized he had gained the upper hand in his dealings with the general.

Geronimo had told Crook that the reason he wanted to stay behind was to gather his followers who lived in remote camps. But Geronimo had other plans. What he really intended to do was raid Mexican ranches for horses, mules, and cattle. When he finally returned to San Carlos, he would bring the herd with him. His plan was to ultimately sell the livestock to the reservation's Apache in order to provide himself with plenty of spending money.

All of this took much longer than "two moons." It was late in February 1884 when Crook received news that Geronimo and his band were finally heading north out of Mexico and approaching the border. He and his followers were driving an enormous herd of cattle they had stolen. However, not long after they reached the reservation, the cattle were taken from Geronimo despite his angry protests, and they were eventually sold by the federal government. The money realized was given to the Mexican government so that it could be distributed to the original owners of the livestock—if they could be found. Geronimo was furious at the loss.

Peace at San Carlos

Even after Geronimo's less than honorable actions, General Crook was generous to him and his band. He allowed them to settle on the San Carlos Reservation on a site of their own choosing. They picked the land around Turkey Creek, a glorious area of towering pines and clear streams. Low hills rose to the north and south. Wild turkeys, deer, and even bears were there to be hunted. But Turkey Creek did not offer sufficient water to irrigate the land for farming. Geronimo and his people would have to manage as best they could. Despite a poor water supply, Geronimo and his cousin Jason Betzinez were successful in raising potatoes and corn during their first year as farmers. The next year, they planted barley. But Geronimo still had little enthusiasm for farming.

This is a recent photograph of Turkey Creek, a part of the San Carlos Reservation chosen by Geronimo and his followers as their home site. It offered clear streams, tall pines, and abundant game, but lacked enough water to farm successfully.

Whether or not the Indians were happy and successful as farmers, they observed the peace agreement they had made with General Crook. For the next two years, there was no violence. No whites were killed. No ranches were vandalized. No horses were stolen. In a report that he prepared in 1884, General Crook was able to say that "for the first time in the history of that fierce people, every member of the Apache tribe is at peace."

General George Crook (1828–1890)

A farm boy born near Dayton, Ohio, General George Crook is often hailed as the U.S. Army's greatest Indian fighter. But he should be admired more as a humanitarian. During his army career and in the years after, he was always a staunch defender of Indian rights.

After graduating from the U.S. Military Academy in 1852, Crook, a mild-mannered six-foot man, was assigned a tour of duty on the Pacific Coast. There he was involved in clashes with the Pit River Indians along the California-Oregon border. During that time, he came to realize that much of the area's strife was caused by the white people's greed for land.

Civil War troops under Crook's command saw action at the Battle of South Mountain, the Battle of Antietam, the Battle of Chickamauga, and the Second Battle of Bull Run. His assignments after the war took him to places plagued by Indian disturbances. In clashes with the Indians, Crook used new tactics. He believed it was vital to use specially trained Indian scouts to track down other Indians in their mountain hideaways.

In his later years, Crook devoted much of his time toward seeking the relocation of the imprisoned Chiricahua. Ultimately, they were transferred to Fort Sill, Oklahoma, and to land set aside for Native Americans— partly due to Crook's efforts.

General George Crook (second from right) is shown here with (left to right) Generals George Forsyth, Wesley Merritt, Philip H. Sheridan, and George Custer during the Civil War.

CHAPTER 9

Run, Ride, Fight, Hide

Keep the scouts on the renegade trail until the outlaws are killed, captured, or driven to unconditional surrender.

—General George Crook

Despite General Crook's cheery words, trouble loomed. An Apache named Kayihtah was partly to blame. He was much younger than Geronimo and had a history of violent behavior. About three years earlier, he and a number of his followers had come upon a group of White Mountain Apache who were on a hunting expedition. For reasons unknown, Kayihtah and his party killed several of the innocent Indians.

Much later, at an Indian dance on the San Carlos Reservation, Kayihtah boasted of the killings. Worse, he hinted that other raids were to come. The White Mountain Indians were furious. They complained to Lieutenant Britton Davis, who was in charge of the Apache scouts.

Davis was sympathetic toward the White Mountain tribesmen and felt Kayihtah should be made to pay for his crime. He arrested the brazen Apache and had him tried before an Indian jury. Kayihtah was found guilty. It was up to General Crook to decide Kayihtah's fate. He sentenced him to serve three years in the military prison on Alcatraz Island in California's San Francisco Bay.

Geronimo was both angered and alarmed by all of this. He reasoned that if Kayihtah could be sent to prison for

For murdering innocent Native Americans, Kayihtah was arrested and sentenced to a military prison on Alcatraz, an island in the San Francisco Bay, shown here in an 1859 photograph.

some crime that occurred in the distant past, the same could happen to him. Other Apache felt as Geronimo did.

Defiance over Drinking

In addition to General Crook's unpopular sentencing, he also enraged the Apache with another ruling. He declared that he was banning the making and drinking of *tizwin*, an alcoholic beverage, because he was convinced that drinking led to squabbling and violence. The incensed Indians balked at Crook's order. *Tizwin* was as much a part of their culture as the bow and arrow. They had promised the general that they would live in peace with the white Americans—and they were keeping that promise. The white

Tizwin

Tizwin was the alcoholic beverage favored by the Apache. It was relatively low in alcoholic content and made from fermented corn. To prepare a batch of *tizwin*, a quantity of corn was first soaked overnight in water. The soaked corn was then placed into a long grass-lined trench in the ground and covered with a layer of grass and perhaps a blanket or some soil. Twice a day for the next ten days, water was sprinkled over the corn, causing the corn to sprout. The sprouting corn was then removed from the trench, ground into a mash, and boiled for four or five hours. Lastly, the liquid was strained and held for twenty-four hours before the new batch of *tizwin* was ready to drink. In Geronimo's autobiography, he noted that the beverage "was very highly prized by the Indians."

officers and soldiers were able to drink their wine and whiskey. Why shouldn't the Indians be allowed to do the same?

Peace-loving Apache at San Carlos began to feel uneasy. Too many of the tribal members were beginning to defy the authority. *Tizwin* drinking had become more frequent and instances of wife beating, which was also forbidden by General Crook, was on the rise. Whether the *tizwin* contributed to this increase cannot be proven.

However, when a distressed young woman called upon Lieutenant Davis to complain that her husband had severely beaten her with a heavy piece of wood, Davis had the man arrested and then jailed at Fort Apache for two weeks. Not satisfied with just the husband's punishment, Davis also arrested

A photograph from the late 1880s depicts Lieutenant Britton Davis, who commanded the Apache scouts at the San Carlos Reservation and played a key role in bringing about the final surrender of Geronimo.

the Indian who had made the *tizwin* the husband had drunk and also sentenced him to two weeks of jail time at Fort Apache.

Shortly after, two Apache leaders named Chihuahua and Mangus appeared at Davis's tent, demanding that the two men be released. Davis refused, and matters took a turn for the worse. A group of about thirty Apache warriors spent an entire night drinking *tizwin*. Geronimo was among the group. The next day before sunrise, they assembled outside of Davis's tent to talk to him. When Davis came out, Chihuahua, although in a drunken state, reminded the lieutenant that they had kept the peace as they had promised General Crook, but, he said, "Now they were being punished for things they had the right to do so long as they did no harm to others."

Chihuahua kept talking. "We all drank *tizwin* last night, all of us in the tent and outside, except the scouts; and many more. What are you going to do about it? Are you going to put us all in jail? You have no jail big enough even if you could put us all in jail."

Davis stood and listened, his face grim. Chihuahua went on to insist that the treatment of their wives was also none of his business. They were not badly treated when they behaved, he said. But when they would not behave, their husbands had the right to punish them.

Chihuahua, pictured here in a studio portrait, headed a separate band of Apache.

Davis told the group that this was too serious a matter to handle by himself. He said that he planned to report their complaints to General Crook. This rattled the Indians. They remembered what had happened to Kayihtah for his wrongful acts. They, too, could be arrested and sent to jail. Geronimo was also quick to recall how he and the other leaders had been seized at Warm Springs, put in irons, and shipped like cattle to San Carlos.

Geronimo feared that he would be made to undergo such treatment again. He and the other leaders began to think that fleeing the reservation might be their only choice. Two days later, on May 17, 1885, Geronimo led a group of thirty-five warriors and 109 women and children in a getaway. When Davis learned of the breakout, he immediately tried to telegraph the news to Captain Francis Pierce, who was in charge of the reservation. But the Indians had cut the wires of the telegraph line, and it was dead.

Geronimo was also quick to recall how he . . . had been seized at Warm Springs, put in irons, and shipped like cattle to San Carlos.

The escapees headed straight for Mexico. Before they reached the border, they split into two groups. One group headed by a Chiricahua warrior was pursued and attacked by troops commanded by Lieutenant Davis, but they managed to flee across the border. The other group, led by Geronimo, also escaped across the border. Once in Mexico, the two groups reunited.

In Pursuit

Again, General George Crook was assigned to track down Geronimo. Crook appointed Captain Emmet Crawford and Lieutenant Charles Gatewood to lead several groups of Indian scouts into Mexico to pursue the Apache. The General's orders were clear: "Keep the scouts on the renegade trail until the outlaws are killed, captured, or driven to unconditional surrender."

At first, Captain Crawford's scouts were able to follow Geronimo's band with ease. The tracks revealed that he had driven the renegades at a frantic pace. Only once in a trek of almost 150 miles did he let the group stop for food and water. But when Geronimo's party reached the Sierra Madre, the trail

Pictured here in a photograph from the 1880s is Captain Emmet Crawford, the army officer who headed the San Carlos Reservation.

vanished. Crawford's scouts believed that Geronimo had wrapped his horses' hoofs in dried skins, so they left no telltale tracks.

From their mountain base, Geronimo and his warriors turned violent again. They raided at least a dozen widely scattered Mexican settlements—probably for food and horses. The government of Mexico tried to stop the attacks with companies of soldiers known as **Irregulars**, who were led by Mexican Indian guides.

Months went by before Captain Crawford and his scouts were able to pick up Geronimo's trail again. It led to a hidden camp. Attacking the camp, the scouts captured fifteen women and children. But the scouts were on foot. Geronimo and his warriors mounted their swift horses and darted away.

While the captain and lieutenant lagged behind, Crawford's scouts discovered another of Geronimo's camps in Mexico's Sierra Madre a little northeast of the town of Nacori. They encircled the camp and proceeded to move in. Suddenly, Geronimo appeared out of nowhere, whooping and hollering, and led a headlong mounted charge through their ranks. Once again, Geronimo had escaped.

Fighting the U. S. and Mexican Armies

In the weeks that followed, the scouts kept on Geronimo's trail, hardly stopping to rest. Through powerful binoculars,

Geronimo kept watch. He was fully aware that Crawford's scouts were close on his heels. And by now, Geronimo's people were in sad shape. The feet of the women and children were bruised and bleeding. Having run out of food and eaten all of their horses, they were becoming weak from hunger.

Crawford's scouts weren't Geronimo's only worry. His band had also come under attack by Mexican Irregulars. Sometimes his band would skirmish with the Mexicans. Other times, they would flee. "It is senseless to fight when you cannot hope to win," said Geronimo.

On New Year's Day in 1886, Crawford's scouts picked up a fresh trail. It led to the highest and wildest part of the Sierra Madre. When they finally came upon Geronimo's camp, the scouts attacked. Several women were wounded. Others were captured. But again, Geronimo and his band took flight.

A photograph taken in early 1886 shows the bedraggled men, women, and children from Geronimo's camp.

Shortly after, Crawford's scouts caught up with Geronimo again. As they attacked, a column of Mexican troops suddenly appeared upon the scene.

When the Mexican troops sighted Crawford's Indian scouts, they mistook them for Geronimo's Indians, and they started firing.

When Crawford saw what was happening, he jumped up and started waving a white handkerchief as a signal to the Mexicans that the Indians they were shooting at were American soldiers. Then a Mexican bullet struck Crawford in the head. Five days later, the wound proved fatal.

When Crawford fell, his scouts boiled with rage. Guns blazing, they rushed the Mexicans, killing their commander and several officers. That put an end to the fight.

Surrender—Again

As for Geronimo, he was a beaten man. He and his followers were on the brink of starvation. They had been forced to abandon the blankets and warm clothing they needed to live in the high mountains. The U.S. soldiers had the upper hand. By using Apache scouts, they had discovered Geronimo's secret refuge. Geronimo realized his situation was hopeless.

On March 25, 1886, Geronimo and General Crook met at Cañon de los Embudos, about twenty miles south of the border. There, Geronimo surrendered. Under the terms of the agreement the two men worked out, Geronimo and his followers would spend not more than two years in confinement in the East. Their families would join them. After the two years, they would be permitted to return to the San Carlos Reservation. The next day, General Crook left for Fort Bowie. Geronimo and the other Apache were to follow with Lieutenant Marion Maus and the scouts.

This photograph from March 1886 captures the historic conference between Geronimo (at left, wearing bandanna) and General George Crook (at right, in white hat).

As General Crook was making his way toward Fort Bowie, chaos descended upon Maus's encampment. An American **bootlegger** slipped into the camp. He carried bottles of mescal, an alcoholic drink made from a desert plant, to sell to the Indians. Geronimo and many of the other Apache could not resist. They became wildly drunk.

The next morning, on March 28, 1886, Maus learned that Geronimo and forty or so of his followers had stampeded out of camp. Once on the loose, they headed back to the Sierra Madre.

Twice now Geronimo had surrendered in good faith to General Crook. And both times he had ignored his promise and broken free. This time his freedom would be brief.

CHAPTER 10

The Final Surrender

I will quit the warpath and live at peace hereafter.

Once he returned to Fort Bowie, General Crook reported what had taken place at Cañon de los Embudos to General Philip H. Sheridan, the U.S. Army's commander in chief. In a telegraphed message, he told the general that Geronimo and his followers had surrendered. As a part of the surrender terms, the Apache agreed to serve two years in prison. After that, they would return to their reservation.

General Sheridan had no love for the Apache or any other Indians. He rejected the terms of the treaty that had been arranged by General Crook. Sheridan said that the Apache's surrender must be "unconditional." He wanted a total surrender. He was willing to spare their lives, but nothing more.

Crook hardly knew what to do next. But before Crook got a chance to act, he received a message from Lieutenant Maus telling him that Geronimo and

A lithograph from the 1860s pictures General Philip Sheridan, commander in chief of the U.S. Army.

General Philip Sheridan (1831–1888)

"The only good Indian is a dead Indian." That statement was said to have been made by General Philip Sheridan, who was well known as an Indian hater. Although he denied ever saying it, those who knew him had no doubt that he agreed with what the statement said. If he did not utter the exact words, he did say something close to it. In January 1869, the general was at Fort Cobb, Indian Territory. There he happened to meet Toch-a-way, chief of the Comanche Indians. To impress the general, the chief puffed out his chest and announced, "Me Toch-a-way, me good Indian." Sheridan grinned and said, "The only good Indians I ever saw were dead."

Sheridan performed notable service during the Civil War and during the Indian Wars of the Great Plains (although his reputation was tarnished by accusations of racism). He was also instrumental in the development of Yellowstone National Park. It is, however, for his "dead Indian" remark that General Sheridan is often remembered.

This c. 1886 lithograph depicts one of Sheridan's Civil War victories in 1864. It is often claimed that he is the originator of the phrase, "The only good Indian is a dead Indian."

his small group of followers had escaped and disappeared into the mountains.

When Sheridan got this news from Crook, he seethed with anger. A "great disappointment," he called it. He added, "It seems strange that Geronimo and party could have escaped without the knowledge of the scouts." Crook was annoyed to hear that his scouts were being blamed for Geronimo's escape. In his reply to Sheridan, Crook said that the scouts were "thoroughly loyal." He explained that the Apache were so widely scattered about the countryside that it was impossible to keep them all under control.

Change in Command

Sheridan was in no mood for explanations. It was clear to Crook that Sheridan had little faith in him or the methods he had used to subdue the renegades. General Crook asked to be relieved of his command. Sheridan was happy to grant Crook his request. The very next day, Sheridan named General Nelson Miles to replace General Crook. Miles was experienced as an Indian fighter, but he did not have General Crook's understanding of the Apache. And as Geronimo and all other Apache would soon learn, he also lacked Crook's integrity.

General Miles arrived at Fort Apache in April 1886. He immediately began to plan his campaign against Geronimo and put an end to Apache terror.

General Nelson Miles, pictured here in a photograph taken during his time of service in the Civil War, replaced General Crook as the head of Fort Apache and was charged with the duty of capturing Geronimo.

At the time, Geronimo headed a group that included no more than nineteen warriors, plus thirteen women and six children. To hunt him down, General Miles organized a force made up of some five thousand troops, one-fourth of the U.S. Army at the time. Sheridan had no confidence or trust in the Indian scouts. He asked Miles not to use them, and Miles agreed to rely on only a handful of them.

To share information as to the whereabouts of the Apache, Miles set up a series of heliograph stations in the mountains. This was a system of mirrors that could be used to flash coded messages from mountain to mountain. The Apache, who at one time had used smoke signals for communication, had also switched to mirrors by this time.

A 19th-century engraving depicts the mirror signal system used between bands of Apache to report information such as U.S. Army troop movements.

Futile Quest

Before General Miles had completed his preparations, Geronimo and his warriors were on the move, attacking with ferocity both north and south of the border. They sometimes attacked ranches in order to get food, such as cattle. At other times, they "attacked every Mexican found, even if for no other reason than to kill." They were desperate men, caught in a hopeless situation. Geronimo knew that "if we returned to the reservation we would be put in prison and killed; if we stayed in Mexico they would continue to send soldiers to fight us."

Miles's troops pursued Geronimo for months. They covered nearly fourteen hundred miles. At times, the heat was so intense that rifle barrels or anything else made of metal could not be touched without causing a burn. Soldiers' feet blistered. Horses broke down. Sudden and heavy rains pounded the men. Only one-third of the enlisted soldiers managed to endure their grueling assignment without injury.

Then General Miles's luck changed. One night at Fort Apache, during the summer of 1886, Miles held a meeting with a group of Apache warriors. He asked for volunteers to take a message to Geronimo. The once troublesome Kayihtah, weary from the constant fighting and running, said he was ready to aid General Miles. He agreed to take a message to Geronimo but asked that he be able to take a companion

Geronimo was a prisoner of war at the time this photograph was taken. General Nelson Miles nicknamed him the Human Tiger for his tenacity and ferocity.

with him for safety. Miles gave his approval, and Kayihtah chose his close friend Martine to go with him.

General Miles picked Lieutenant Charles Gatewood to lead the mission. The Apache knew and trusted the thirty-three-year-old Gatewood, who had a lot of experience dealing with the tribe. He had also earned a reputation as a man of integrity. To better communicate with the Apache, he had learned their language. Because he wore big shoes, they called him Chief Long Foot.

Charles Gatewood, pictured here in the uniform of a U.S. Military Academy cadet, was trusted by the Apache.

Mounted on mules, Gatewood's party included Kayihtah and Martine, who were expected to handle initial dealings with Geronimo. With the scouts leading the way, they headed straight for the Mexican border.

Surrender at Last

Not long after they had crossed into Mexico, Gatewood learned that Geronimo and his band were camped in the mountains near Fronteras, Mexico, only about thirty miles directly south of Douglas, Arizona. Gatewood hurried to Fronteras. There, he heard that two women from Geronimo's band had come to town to buy food and mescal.

Gatewood set up camp east of Fronteras on the banks of the Río Bavispe. Kayihtah, Martine, and a handful of scouts were sent to follow the tracks of the women. Within three days, they discovered what they believed to be Geronimo's hideout. It was perched high in Torres Mountains on a peak that the Apache called "Mountain Tall."

Leaving the rest of the group behind, Kayihtah and Martine climbed the steep mountain. As they approached the summit, they didn't know what to expect. Would they be looked upon as traitors? Their legs trembled with fear. To their relief, they were greeted warmly. Even Geronimo seemed happy to see them. After some friendly conversation, Kayihtah delivered the message he carried from General Miles: The general wanted Geronimo and his followers to give themselves up.

Kayihtah and Martine were brave Apache army scouts who played a vital role in Geronimo's capture and final surrender.

Silence greeted Kayihtah's words. Geronimo's half brother White Horse was the first to speak. "I am going to surrender," he said. "My wife and children have been captured. I love them, and want to be with them."

A second brother announced that if White Horse surrendered, he would surrender, too. Moments later, the third and youngest brother made a statement that was much the same. Then a somber Geronimo spoke. "I have been depending heavily on you three men. You have been great fighters in battle. If you are going to surrender, there is no use my going without you, I will give up with you."

But Geronimo was taking no chances. He held Kayihtah as a hostage while Martine went back to tell Gatewood that

Geronimo was willing to talk. Geronimo eventually met with Gatewood, who promised to arrange a meeting between Geronimo and General Miles. It was held early in September 1886 at Skeleton Canyon.

Too Good to Be True

When they met, General Miles began by saying, "The President of the United States has sent me to speak to you. He has heard of your trouble with the white men, and says that if you will agree to a few words of treaty we need have no more trouble." Geronimo asked General Miles what the treaty terms were to be. According to Geronimo, the general replied: "I will take you under government protection; I will build you a house; I will fence you much land; I will give you cattle, horses, mules, and farming implements. You will be furnished with men to work the farm, for you yourself will not have to work. In the fall, I will send you blankets and clothing so that you will not suffer from cold in the winter time."

The general wanted Geronimo and his followers to give themselves up.

Although Geronimo was pleased with the treaty, he told Miles he had heard such offers before, which turned out to be lies. But Miles said, "This time it is the truth." Upon hearing that, Geronimo agreed to the treaty. "I will quit the warpath and live at peace hereafter," he said.

Then General Miles reached down and with his bare hand swept clean a spot of dusty ground. As he did so, he said, "Your past deeds shall be wiped out like this and you will start a new life." Geronimo felt a wave of relief sweep over him. There had been no talk of going to prison.

This monument stands in Skeleton Canyon, Arizona, located in the southeastern corner of the state, and marks the spot of Geronimo's capture.

The surrender of Geronimo and his warriors at Skeleton Canyon in 1886 brought to an end the one-hundred-year struggle by the Apache to defend their homeland. "GERONIMO CAPTURED!" "APACHE WAR ENDED!" screamed newspaper headlines. The raiding and killing were over. The people of Arizona and New Mexico could rejoice.

But for Geronimo and all other Apache, there would be no joy. The promises made by General Miles were never kept. The federal government never intended to keep them. Miles had lied in order to get Geronimo to surrender. Afterward, the days of the Apache would be filled with sadness and despair.

Prisoner of War

We had no property, and I looked in vain for General Miles to send me to that land of which he had spoken.

Geronimo was in his mid-fifties when he agreed to abandon his life as a renegade. He was to spend his next twenty-three years as a prisoner of war and, as such, was kept under guard and confined by the United States government. Geronimo never saw his homeland again.

In a well-known photograph from 1886, Geronimo (seated in the front row, third from the right) and other Apache prisoners of war pose at the rest stop on their way to internment.

About 400 Apache men, women, and children, described as "hostiles" by the army, were sent as prisoners of war to Fort Marion in St. Augustine, Florida, seen here in a general view.

Like Geronimo, hundreds of peaceful Indians living on the San Carlos Reservation were treated in the same deplorable manner. They included about seventy men and 325 women and children.

Many of the men had served as scouts, helping federal troops find the Apache who were described as "hostiles." The scouts were shipped to Fort Marion in Florida, where they shared a long stretch of fenced-in living along with the "outlaw" Indians. Even Kayihtah and Martine, who had risked their lives guiding Lieutenant Gatewood on the way to Geronimo's mountain hideout, were seized and thrown in with the other prisoners. They, too, ended up at Fort Marion.

As for Geronimo and his band, authorities in Washington, D.C., ordered Miles to hold them in local jails until government officials could decide what to do with them. General Miles knew that the people of Arizona were in a vengeful mood. They could hardly wait to get their hands on Geronimo and his followers. Any trial, Miles told his superiors, would be "simply a mockery of justice."

A New Life

Miles felt that Geronimo and his people were in jeopardy and needed to get out of Arizona as quickly as possible. As soon as he had the chance, the general placed Geronimo and his followers on a train bound for Fort Marion. But before they ever got there, new orders came down from Washington, D.C. Geronimo and his followers were to be sent to Fort Pickens on Santa Rosa Island at the entrance to Florida's Pensacola Bay.

They arrived there on October 25, 1886. One of the biggest forts that protected Pensacola Harbor, Fort Pickens played an active role in the Civil War. But in the years after, it had been allowed to fall into decay and ruin. Largely uninhabited, the huge open area where soldiers had once paraded was now overgrown with weeds and small trees. On the island's southern flank, thick-walled masonry chambers had been built to house the fort's huge cannons. These structures, called casemates, were to serve as living quarters for the prisoners.

Grass and small shrubs were growing over and out of the casemates. A small pine tree was sprouting out of one of the

A hand-colored Currier & Ives print dating to the 1860s pictures Fort Pickens, located in the harbor of Pensacola, Florida, where Geronimo and his people were first held as prisoners of war.

chimneys. Geronimo and the others were kept busy pulling weeds, clearing out the overspreading growth, and cleaning and scrubbing, in an effort to make the buildings livable. They worked five days a week, six hours a day.

A Pensacola newspaper reporter, on a visit to the fort, noted that Geronimo held his usual status as a leader and was obeyed by the others.

The reporter also mentioned Geronimo's "cruel countenance." He said, "Geronimo's face is expressive of [intelligence], but he has the coldest eye we have ever beheld in the face of a human being." However, it is easy to understand why Geronimo did not appear warm and charming. At that time, while he and the other Apache men were assigned to Fort Pickens, their wives and children were shipped to Fort Marion. Geronimo and the others longed to see their families.

This photograph, dating to 1904, shows a grim-faced Geronimo during the time he was being held as a prisoner of war.

As more and more newspaper articles documented the plight of these Indians, white Americans became aware of how poorly the Apache were being treated by the federal government. Even President Grover Cleveland came to realize that the Fort Pickens Apache were cruelly being forced to live apart from their families.

Family Reunion

With so much attention focused on the problem, the government finally agreed that the system in place was unjust. No longer would family members be separated. It is believed that three of Geronimo's wives and several of his children were reunited with him at Fort Pickens. The children included a young son, Fenton, and an infant daughter, Lenna, whom he had never seen before.

Geronimo and his wives and children settled into one of the fort's casemates. The women cared for the children and performed household chores. Geronimo continued to work with the other men in clearing the parade grounds and digging wells. They clung to the hope that one day they would win their freedom and be able to return to their homeland.

While life seemed serene at Fort Pickens, the federal government was having serious problems at Fort Marion. Nearly 350 Apache lived there. Overcrowding along with the humid climate made life hard to bear. **Malaria** and other diseases took a heavy toll. Sanitation was primitive. Malnutrition was rampant.

Public pressure eventually forced the federal government to seek some other location for the Apache. An old U.S. Army ammunition plant near Mount Vernon, Alabama, was chosen as the site. It was located on a plateau above the Mobile River, about thirty miles inland from the Gulf of Mexico. The plant, which dated back to 1828, was given the name Mount Vernon Barracks. In 1887 and 1888, the Fort Marion Apache were moved to the Mount Vernon site.

They clung to the hope that one day they would win their freedom and be able to return to their homeland.

Relocation

Once the Fort Marion Apache were settled at Mount Vernon Barracks, the government, in a cost-saving move, decided to send Geronimo, his family, and the other Apache there. They were taken from Fort Pickens in May 1888 and placed aboard a train bound for Mount Vernon, which was less than one hundred miles north and west of Fort Pickens.

When Geronimo and his party arrived at the barracks, no one was there to meet them. They stared anxiously at the cluster of log cabins beyond the gate. The door of one of the cabins opened and a woman came out. As she made her way toward the group, Geronimo recognized her as his twenty-one-year-old daughter, Lulu. They had been separated following Geronimo's final surrender. Lulu ran to Geronimo and threw her arms about him and wept.

Living conditions at the Mount Vernon Barracks were even worse than what Geronimo and his people had experienced at Fort Pickens. They were ravaged by **tuberculosis** and other illnesses. Hordes of mosquitoes added to their suffering. It rained frequently and cabin roofs leaked. Because of the dampness, mold

In a photograph from the late 1880s, Geronimo (at the far right) poses with his fellow Apache tribesmen at Mount Vernon Barracks in Mount Vernon, Alabama—their place of confinement as prisoners of war beginning in 1888.

clung to cabin walls and everyone's food and clothing. During the Apache's first eight months at Mount Vernon, two men, ten women, and nine children died. One of Geronimo's wives was among the many Apache who died. He was also separated from another wife, who for reasons of health, had to leave for the Mescalero Apache Reservation in New Mexico, where the air was much drier. Two of their small children, including Lenna, later joined her.

Living under such terrible conditions, Geronimo's thoughts sometimes returned to the peace treaty he had made with General Miles many years before. "We had no property, and I looked in vain for General Miles to send me to that land of which he had spoken," Geronimo said. "I longed in vain for the implements, house, and stock that General Miles had promised me."

Despite the broken promises and daily hardships, Geronimo managed to adapt during his years at Mount Vernon. Although he was still a leader within his community, he now found different roles to play. When a school established by a church group began operating at Mount Vernon, Geronimo contributed to its success. From eight to eleven o'clock each morning, the school's two teachers taught arithmetic, reading, spelling, and geography. The young Apache were also schooled in English as a second language and in gymnastics. Geronimo served as the school's disciplinarian. He called the children to class with a big cowbell and he monitored classroom conduct. He performed his tasks so effectively that school officials awarded him a silver medal.

Mount Vernon Celebrity

Day in and day out, a steady stream of tourists visited the Mount Vernon Apache. They were brought to the site by a train from Mobile, thirty miles to the south. Many of the visitors were surprised to see the Indians were not held in prison cells, but instead had the freedom to move about the camp.

As the sightseers toured the site, Apache families stood in front of their cabins and smiled politely. They offered to sell the bows and arrows and beaded purses they had made and earned a profit doing so.

Geronimo himself became a special attraction. No longer was he the greatly feared Apache warrior. He was now a famous person, and a friendly one, at that. He had learned to write his name. He had also learned that tourists were willing to pay for his autograph. For a fee that sometimes reached as much as twenty-five cents, an amount equivalent to several dollars by today's standards, he would slowly print "GERONIMO" on a small white card.

GERONIMO

Geronimo happily sold his autograph, shown here, to admirers and tourists for up to 25 cents.

Once, a reporter spotted Geronimo seated in front of his cabin. He was busy decorating a whip with colored beads. Undoubtedly, it was meant to be sold to the tourists. The celebrity Apache was wearing an overcoat with a bright red lining. "His favorite **squaw**," the reporter said, "sits at his feet, almost invariably cooking pumpkins, for which her master has an insatiable appetite."

Geronimo poses with one of the several women he married during his long life.

Life at Mount Vernon

In May 1890, the *New York Times* sent a correspondent to Mount Vernon Barracks to report on how the Apache prisoners of war were getting along. At the time, Geronimo was beginning his third year at the site.

Mount Vernon was made up of about one hundred cabins and a few scattered tepees. Each cabin had two rooms that were joined by a small courtyard open to the sky. A fire for cooking was built in the courtyard.

Each cabin was occupied by a family, which usually consisted of a husband, two or three wives, and an assortment of babies and children, who played outside the cabin.

The women at Mount Vernon performed a variety of tasks. They were responsible for fetching water and firewood, preparing food, and bathing their children.

The children went to school each morning from eight to eleven. "In the afternoon," said the reporter, "there is a singing school for the children, which has been of untold benefit in enlarging their vocabulary in a pleasant manner."

This article from the *New York Times* of May 11, 1890, gave readers a rare view of Geronimo and his fellow prisoners of war during their stay at Mount Vernon Barracks.

GERONIMO'S ALABAMA CAMP.

THE CHIRICAHUAS AND THEIR CABINS
AT MOUNT VERNON BARRACKS.

To the Editor of the New-York Times:

It would be difficult to find anything more picturesque and interesting than is the camp of the Chiricahua Apache Indians now held as prisoners of war at Mount Vernon Barracks, Alabama. It consists of a hundred or more cabins and a few scattered wigwams, which the older women have been unable to abandon. Geronimo, who foiled our army again and again, is seated in front of his cabin, beading a whip, and with an overcoat on, the cape of which is lined with the artillery red; nor has he so far neglected artistic effect as not to have the most perfect harmony exist between the lining of the cape and his complexion. His favorite squaw sits at his feet, almost invariably cooking pumpkins, for which her master has an insatiable appetite. Not far off is Na-chiz with the yellow of the cavalry, and few cavalrymen could wear it with more military grace and dignity than does he.

Groups of boys are playing marbles, their long, black hair set off by a bright red jerkin, or a hat with a gorgeous piece of calico tied around it and ornamented with numerous white pins. Perhaps they still cling to Apache taste and wear a feather. Their trousers require frequent pulls to keep them from taking French leave, and, indeed, one small urchin has evidently either not had time to make his morning toilet or else regards clothes as an absurd idiosyncrasy of civilization, for his sole adornment is a necktie. The girls, with gowns appallingly décolletées, but decked with beads and charms innumerable, scorn so infantile an amusement as marbles, and are frequently seen gambling away their ornaments with as much, if not more, zeal than their mothers could. The women are performing every kind of work, fetching wood and water, preparing the food, scrubbing their unfortunate children in the open air, or washing their own hair; others have obviously concluded that cleanliness is indeed godliness, and for the first time probably in six months everything wearable within their reach is in the washtub; three or four shivering youngsters, almost, if not quite, nude, stand waiting until their clothes shall be ready, which they will put on—still wet.

The cabins have as a rule two floored rooms, joined by a kind of inclosed court, in the middle of which the fire is built; the smoke is usually so dense that it requires several moments for one's eyes to become sufficiently accustomed to it to discern the objects around one. When at length the smoky fog lifts a little, two squaws can be seen gambling in one corner, while a third is making bread. The master is seated in the one chair, half asleep, and the babies are conveniently disposed of in their baskets standing against the wall. The raw beef is hanging up to dry and does not much improve the unpleasant odor that prevails. Calm contentment apparently reigns, which is really remarkable when one considers that a man frequently has two, and sometimes three, wives living in the same cabin.

Much is being done for the civilization and improvement of the Apache. Every morning from 8 to 11 the children are instructed, and later the men. In the afternoon there is a singing school for the children, which has been of untold benefit in enlarging their vocabulary in a pleasant manner.

A bathhouse has lately been established by the children's teacher, and, although it was at first thought to be quite impracticable, has proved the reverse, as on the first Saturday that it was in working order some twenty boys and six or or seven women, with their smaller children, appeared eager to begin work. The chief difficulty is that all wish to take the bath, and then, with their clothes tied up in the towel, return home to dress. VAILLANT JULICO.

A Special Visitor

In 1889, General Oliver O. Howard visited the Mount Vernon Barracks. Geronimo had warm memories of the general from his days at Apache Pass. "We never had so good a friend among the United States officers as General Howard," Geronimo had said of him. When the general arrived at Mount Vernon, Geronimo was the first person he saw. He was sitting before a bundle of painted canes that he had crafted from small tree limbs for sale to sightseers. When he spotted General Howard, he handed the

General Oliver O. Howard, who lost his arm fighting for the Union in the Civil War, is pictured here in a photograph that dates to 1908. He visited Mount Vernon Barracks in 1889, where he met Geronimo once again.

canes to a friend and ran to meet him and hugged him twice. Since he wanted to be sure that the General knew who he was, he kept shouting his name, "Geronimo! Geronimo!"

The old Apache leader then ran to get an interpreter so he could talk to the general. He told Howard that he was now a school superintendent and that the children were taught by "fine lady teachers." Perhaps in an effort to please General Howard, Geronimo also said to him, "All the children go to their school. I make them. I want them to be white children."

Although Geronimo tried to give the impression that he was contented, it became obvious to General Howard that he still clung to the hope of returning to the Apache homeland. "Indians sick here," Geronimo said. "Air bad and water bad." Geronimo begged General Howard to speak to the president on his behalf. For his part, the general tried to

Although Geronimo tried to give the impression that he was contented, it became obvious to General Howard that he still clung to the hope of returning to the Apache homeland.

make Geronimo understand that the people of Arizona still remembered the many cruelties they had suffered at the hands of the Apache. Their feeling of hate still ran deep. If the Apache went back to the Chiricahua Mountains, they were sure to be the target of terrible violence. For now, Geronimo had to remain where he was.

CHAPTER 12

Final Days

I do not consider that I am an Indian any more. I am a white man. . . . I consider that all white men are my brothers and all white women are now my sisters.

When Geronimo and his followers were taken to Mount Vernon Barracks in 1888, their stay there was supposed to be a short one. It didn't turn out that way. Government officials weren't able to decide upon a permanent home for what they now called "Geronimo's Apache." These Indians, Geronimo included, remained at Mount Vernon Barracks for close to seven years. Geronimo, nearing his seventies, along with his followers, had accepted the fact that they would remain under the control and care of federal government. They could do nothing about it.

One or two individuals did try. Before his death, General Crook had favored the idea of creating a homeland for the Apache on a government reservation at Fort Sill in the Oklahoma Territory. Fort Sill had plenty of room. Some of it was pastureland suitable for cattle. It also had countless acres of timber that could be used for firewood or building homes.

However, there was strong opposition to the idea. A U.S. Army cavalry post in southwestern Oklahoma, Fort Sill was said by many to be too close to Arizona and New Mexico. It was feared that the Apache might again terrorize

General Crook supported moving the Apache to Fort Sill in the Oklahoma Territory, where there was plenty of space for the people. The fort is photographed here in 1889.

the people in those two territories. When General Crook died in 1890, the effort to move to Fort Sill stalled. Three years later, General Miles came forward to support the plan to shift the Apache to Fort Sill.

Geronimo liked the idea, and in an effort to convince others said, "I do not consider that I am an Indian any more. I am a white man. . . . I consider that all white men are my brothers, and all white women are now my sisters."

Coming from Geronimo, that was a remarkable statement, and some whites were skeptical and scoffed at it. But it was evidence as to how well he had adjusted to life in the custody of the federal government. The years to come would offer further proof of Geronimo's sincerity.

A Permanent Home

Late in 1894, final plans were drawn for the federal government to officially relocate the various Apache tribes to

Fort Sill. A reservation for them would be carved from Fort Sill's wide-open spaces. They would still be considered prisoners of war by the federal government, however.

The Apache arrived at Fort Sill early in October that year. Since winter weather was approaching, they made no attempt to build houses. Instead, they lived in wickiups, which were erected by the women. In place of branches for covering, they used sheets of canvas provided by the army.

In the spring, following an Apache custom, the Indians formed themselves into groups, which were designated into small villages throughout the reservation. Geronimo and other

Apache wickiups were traditionally covered with small branches, vines, and grass, but the army at Fort Sill provided sheets of canvas for the Apache to use as roofing. This 1939 photo shows some Apache in front of their canvas-covered wickiup.

Dressed for her womanhood ceremony, Geronimo's daughter, Eva (right), sixteen years old at the time, poses with Ramona Daklugie, Geronimo's niece.

tribal leaders each headed a group. Geronimo's group included his wife, Ziyeh, and their two small children, a son, Fenton, and a daughter, Eva, who was five.

The Apache were taught by the army how to build wood-frame cabins that had four walls and slanted roofs. Each group had its own plot of several acres of land to farm. Melons and cantaloupes were popular crops.

Geronimo, who in the past took no pleasure in farming, now approached farm tasks with enthusiasm. He raised mostly melons and corn, and beds of flowers encircled his house. He became one of the reservation's better farmers and was undoubtedly motivated by the fact that there was money to be made. The government agreed to buy whatever foodstuffs the Apache themselves were unable to consume.

A photograph from the 1890s pictures the entrance to a Fort Sill home, showing Indian trophies and animal skins.

Because his wife, Ziyeh, was in poor health, suffering from tuberculosis, Geronimo did the household chores as well. He cooked the meals, washed the dishes, and kept the house tidy. Once, when a visitor tracked in some dirt, Geronimo gave him an angry look. Then he grabbed a broom and swept the floor clean. Ziyeh died in 1904. Geronimo married again the next year, but the marriage failed to last.

A Person of Renown

By the time Geronimo had arrived at Fort Sill, he was already a celebrity. In fact, on the journey from Mount Vernon Barracks to Fort Sill, gleeful crowds turned out at stops along the way to get a look at the old Apache. They broke into cheers when he appeared before them.

During the many years he spent at Fort Sill, Geronimo's popularity grew by leaps and bounds. Tourists loved him. They paid him to pose for pictures or for any scrap of paper bearing his autograph. Some just wanted to gaze upon him. Artists asked him to pose for portraits. Historians were eager to record his thoughts about his reign as a warrior leader. Writers for the popular press of the day wanted tales of Geronimo's acts of savagery. If he didn't tell them any, they sometimes made them up.

A writer once asked Geronimo to show him his coat made out of ninety-nine scalps. Geronimo had no such coat. It was not generally the custom of the Apache to scalp their victims. Geronimo didn't know what to say. When the writer asked a second time, Geronimo turned and walked away.

During the many years he spent at Fort Sill, Geronimo's popularity grew by leaps and bounds.

Another writer, gathering information for a book, recalled meeting Geronimo in 1905. The smiling warrior wore a blue cloth coat, and the writer found that "while he was quick to understand much that was said to him, he spoke but a few words of English." For any lengthy interview, Geronimo called upon an interpreter.

Geronimo continued to enjoy enormous popularity everywhere he traveled. Since he was still officially a prisoner of war, he needed special permission from the government for any public appearances outside of Oklahoma. Armed guards often traveled with him.

Geronimo sometimes appeared at state fairs and **expositions**. Held annually, such events offered a wide array of attractions for the many thousands who attended. There were impressive exhibitions of farm produce and livestock. Also, parades, music,

When posing for photographs, Geronimo was often asked to put on feathered headgear or wear other popular badges of Indian culture, which he was usually willing to do, even though they were not authentic forms of Apache dress.

vendors, riders, crafts, and sometimes nightly fireworks thrilled the many visitors. At the Trans-Mississippi and International Exposition of 1898 in Omaha, Nebraska, Geronimo was the chief attraction. When his train made stops on the way to Omaha, huge crowds mobbed him at the station platform, hoping to catch a glimpse of the famous Indian. He happily sold the buttons from his coat for twenty-five cents apiece and his hat for five dollars to grateful admirers. As the train moved on to the next station, Geronimo would sew more buttons on his coat for sale at the next stop—and put on another hat from the supply he carried.

A Reunion with General Miles

One of the many visitors to the exposition was General Nelson Miles. Geronimo had not seen the general for twelve years, since their fateful meeting at Skeleton Canyon where Geronimo had finally surrendered. When the two men sat face to face, Geronimo was jittery, for he planned to confront the general. Sweat trickled down his face. He had trouble getting his words out.

But he clearly remembered the promises that General Miles had made to him. They were promises that were never kept.

Geronimo accused the general of lying to him. Miles merely grinned and said that he learned to lie from Geronimo, who had promised so many times to live in peace, but did not. "You lied to Mexicans, Americans, and to your own Apaches, for thirty years. White men only lied to you once, and I did it."

Miles . . . said that he learned to lie from Geronimo, who had promised so many times to live in peace, but did not.

Geronimo had no answer for that. He then made a request. He told General Miles that he wanted to return to Arizona where the "acorns and piñon nuts, the quail and the wild turkey, the giant cactus and the palo verdes . . . all miss me . . . [and] I miss them, too. I want to go back to them."

The general shrugged. "[The] men and women who live in Arizona, they do not miss you . . . ," the general said. "Folks in Arizona sleep now at night, [for now they] have no fear that Geronimo will come and kill them." General Miles made it clear to Geronimo that the trees and mountains would have to get along without him.

In the years that followed, Geronimo kept busy. He appeared at the Pan-American Exposition in Buffalo, New York, in the summer of 1901. He was later a guest at the Louisiana Purchase Exposition in St. Louis, Missouri, in 1904. At both sites, Geronimo sold bows and arrows he had made as well as autographs and photographs. An official at the St. Louis fair found Geronimo to be "an agreeable, amiable old man, and happy as a bird." Geronimo's joy may have been due, at least in part, from the money he was earning. "When I returned I had plenty of money— more than I had ever owned before."

Geronimo demonstrates one of his handcrafted bow-and-arrow sets, which he sold to admiring fans during his public appearances.

Now a celebrity, Geronimo poses with two unidentified men at the Pan-American Exhibition in Buffalo, New York, in the summer of 1901.

A Tragic End

According to Jason Betzinez, Geronimo's cousin, the old Apache always had a weakness for liquor. One day in 1909, Geronimo, who was now well into his eighties, went to town and bought some liquor to drink. He got drunk and started home after dark. Riding through the cold and rainy night, he fell off his horse and lay on the ground until morning. He quickly caught pneumonia, and a few days later, the infection took Geronimo's life. He died at the Indian hospital at Fort Sill on February 17.

Geronimo's relatives and fellow tribesmen buried him at the Fort Sill Indian cemetery created for Apache prisoners of war. His grave, later to be marked by a stone pyramid, is still there today.

This modern photograph shows the Fort Sill gravesites of Geronimo, his wife, Ziyeh, and their daughter, Eva.

In 1912, the Apache at Fort Sill got their freedom. Congress passed a law releasing them as prisoners of war. Some 187 of the Fort Sill Apache made the decision to live on the Mescalero Apache Reservation in south-central New Mexico. When the group arrived at their new home in 1913, the Mescalero Apache welcomed them. Kayihtah and Martine were among the new arrivals. Seventy-eight Fort Sill Apache preferred to remain in Oklahoma. The government purchased farms for them near the town of Apache, just north of Fort Sill.

Recasting the Past

During much of his life, Geronimo was feared and hated by white people of the Southwest for his countless acts of terrorism.

They looked upon him as a bloodthirsty savage. Because of the cruelties that he and his followers inflicted upon Mexicans and white Americans, and because of their years of defiance of the federal government, virtually all Apache came to be looked upon with contempt. As a result, many members of Geronimo's own tribe had little use for him.

Today, however, Geronimo is seldom thought of in those terms. At his burial, the Reverend Leonard L. Legters of the Apache Reformed Church noted that Geronimo "had doubtless been the greatest war leader American Indians had ever known."

Since that time, Geronimo's reputation as a courageous warrior has grown. There is nothing but admiration for him. His cruelties are usually overlooked. Hollywood has contributed to this change. The many feature films and made-for-TV movies about Geronimo mix fact with fiction. In these, Geronimo has usually been portrayed as a valiant Apache who spent his years defending his home, family, and way of life.

Geronimo's name is well known today. Memorials in his honor dot the Southwest. In Arizona, Oklahoma, and Texas, towns have been named for him. Countless pubs and restaurants throughout the United States bear his name.

Chuck Connors portrayed Geronimo in one of the many motion pictures and television presentations in recent decades that have been based on the life of the Apache leader. This 1962 photograph shows the actor in costume for the role.

Towns in Arizona, Oklahoma, and Texas have been named for Geronimo, as have countless other places, people, and things in the United States.

On Geronimo Road at Fort Sill stands the Geronimo Road Elementary School.

Geronimo's name is sometimes linked with that of such revolutionaries as Ernesto "Che" Guevara and Marcos. Che Guevara, a Cuban **guerrilla** of the late 1950s, was the leader of an independent force seeking to overthrow the existing power structure. Marcos is the spokesperson for the Mexican rebel movement.

Geronimo's story has taken on the qualities of a legend. He has been glorified as a freedom fighter, a product of the noble Apache culture. Reality has been thrust aside. Like Daniel Boone and Davy Crockett, like Annie Oakley and Billy the Kid, Geronimo's story has been romanticized, and he has become an American folk hero. History has been reshaped. Geronimo himself, never one to be troubled by guilt, would see nothing wrong with that.

Geronimo poses in a hand-colored version of a popular portrait of the Apache warrior, taken in the late 1880s.

"Geronimo!" the Yell

Geronimo's name is well known today. One reason is an incident that took place in 1940, not long before America's entry into World War II. A unit of paratroopers at Fort Benning, Georgia, was beginning a risky training mission, and the troops were jittery. To calm their nerves, they went to a movie the night before the jump. The movie was *Geronimo*. On their way back to camp, Private Aubrey Eberhardt announced that he had no fear of the next day's jump. His buddies didn't believe him. They said he'd be so scared he probably wouldn't remember his name.

To demonstrate that he could keep a cool head, he told his buddies that when he jumped, he would remember to yell another person's name—Geronimo. And that's exactly what he did. When he jumped out of the plane, he cried out, "Geronimo!" with an earsplitting scream. Even the men on the field below heard it.

In the days that followed, Eberhardt's buddies took up the cry. It lived on as the unofficial yell of U.S. airborne troops and continues to this day to be used by civilian parachutists and skydivers.

In a photograph taken during a training exercise at Fort Benning, Georgia, in 1943, army parachutists leap from their aircraft, presumably shouting, "Geronimo!" as they go.

Glossary

adobe—sun-dried brick or building made of clay and straw.

bootlegger—someone who makes or sells liquor illegally.

buckskin—the skin of a male animal, usually a male deer.

cavalry—the part of an army made up of soldiers trained to fight on horseback.

contiguous—sharing an edge or boundary; touching.

expositions—public shows or exhibitions.

guerrilla—a member of an irregular group of soldiers engaging in tactics such as surprise raids and sabotage.

Irregulars—convicts released from prisons who were given arms and supplies, then led by Mexican Indians into the mountains to fight.

malaria—a disease carried by mosquitoes that causes chills and fever and sometimes death.

marauding—raiding and plundering.

pony express—a system of delivering mail in the early 1860s by riders using fast ponies and horses.

prophecy—a prediction of what is to come.

renegade—someone who chooses to live outside laws or conventions.

squaw—a disparaging term used to describe an American Indian woman.

tepee—an American Indian dwelling made of animal hides placed over a cone-shaped frame of long poles.

tosch—a special type of baby cradle used by American Indians, also known as a cradleboard.

tuberculosis—a disease that can affect many tissues of the body, but mainly the lungs, and was sometimes fatal in Geronimo's day.

Bibliography

Books

Betzinez, Jason with Wilbur Sturtevant Nye. *I Fought with Geronimo*. Harrisburg, PA: Stackpole Books, 1959.

Bourke, John G. *On the Border with Crook*. Lincoln: University of Nebraska Press, 1971.

Brinkley, Alan. *The Unfinished Nation: A Concise History of the American People, Vol. 1*. New York: McGraw Hill, 2008.

Brinkley, Alan. *The Unfinished Nation: A Concise History of the American People, Vol. 2*. New York: McGraw Hill, 2008.

Davis, Britton. *The Truth About Geronimo*. Lincoln: University of Nebraska Press, 1976.

Debo, Angie. *Geronimo: The Man, His Time, His Place*. Norman, OK: University of Oklahoma Press, 1976.

Ellis, Edward S. *The History of Our Country: From the Discovery of America to the Present Time*. Cincinatti, OH: Jones Brothers, 1900.

Etulain, Richard W. and Glenda Riley. *Chiefs and Generals: Nine Men Who Shaped the American West*. Golden, CO: Fulcrum Publishing, 2004.

Geronimo, as told to S. M. Barrett. *Geronimo: His Own Story: The Autobiography of a Great Patriot Warrior*. New York: Penguin Books, 1996.

Howard, Oliver Otis. *Famous Indian Chiefs I Have Known*. Lincoln: University of Nebraska Press, 1989.

Moody, Ralph. *Geronimo: Wolf of the Warpath*. New York: Sterling Publishing, 1976.

Shorto, Russell. *Geronimo and the Struggle for Apache Freedom*. Englewood Cliffs, NJ: Silver Burdett Press, 1989.

Worcester, Donald E. *The Apaches: Eagles of the Southwest*. Norman, OK: University of Oklahoma Press, 1979.

Articles

Mieder, Wolfgang. "'The Only Good Indian Is a Dead Indian': History and Meaning of a Proverbial Stereotype." *The Journal of American Folklore* 106, no. 419 (Winter 1993): 38–60.

Valliant, Julico. "Geronimo's Alabama Camp: The Chiricauhuas and Their Cabins at Mount Vernon Barracks." *The New York Times*, May 11, 1890.

Source Notes

The following list identifies the sources of the quoted material found in this book. The first and last few words of each quotation are cited, followed by the source. Complete information on each source can be found in the Bibliography.

Abbreviations:
AES—*The Apaches: Eagles of the Southwest*
CG—*Chiefs and Generals: Nine Men Who Shaped the American West*
FIC—*Famous Indian Chiefs I Have Known*
GHOS—*Geronimo: His Own Story: The Autobiography of a Great Patriot Warrior*
GMTP—*Geronimo: The Man, His Time, His Place*
GWW—*Geronimo: Wolf of the Warpath*
HOC—*The History of Our Country: From the Discovery of America to the Present Time*
IFG—*I Fought with Geronimo*
NYT—*The New York Times* article
OBC—*On the Border with Crook*
OGI—"The Only Good Indian Is a Dead Indian"
TAG—*The Truth About Geronimo*

INTRODUCTION: Full of Vengeance
   PAGE 1 *"I could not . . . in this revenge.":* GHOS, p. 78
   PAGE 1 *"I had lost all.":* GHOS p. 78

CHAPTER 1: Apache Boyhood
   PAGE 2 *"This range . . . burial places.":* GHOS, p. 58
   PAGE 2 *"near the . . . Arizona.":* GMTP, p. 7
   PAGE 4 *"fourth in . . . girls.":* GHOS, p. 58
   PAGE 4 *"As a babe . . . Indian babes.":* GHOS, p. 59
   PAGES 4–5 *"Sometimes . . . we would hide . . . many hours.":* GHOS, p. 59
   PAGE 5 *"When the crops . . . over the field.":* GHOS, p. 59, 60
   PAGE 5 *"No boy . . . they did so.":* GHOS, p. 60
   PAGE 5 *"for strength . . . and protection.":* GHOS, p. 59
   PAGE 7 *"My son . . . with them.":* GHOS, p. 18
   PAGE 8 *"It required more . . . any other animal.":* GHOS, p. 67
   PAGE 9 *"Usen did . . . to be eaten.":* GHOS, p. 68

PAGE 110 *"while he was . . . of English.":* GMTP, p. 387
PAGE 111 *"You lied to . . . and I did it.":* GMTP, p. 405
PAGE 112 *"acorns and piñon . . . back to them.":* GMTP, p. 405
PAGE 112 *"[The] men and . . . kill them.":* GMTP, p. 406
PAGE 112 *"an agreeable, amiable . . . a bird.":* CG, p. 100
PAGE 112 *"When I returned . . . before.":* GHOS, p. 155
PAGE 115 *"had doubtless . . . ever known.":* CG, p. 85

Image Credits

About the Author

George Sullivan writes books of facts, history, and biography for children and young adults. His titles cover a wide range of subjects, from aviation to archaeology, from baseball to witchcraft. He has written young adult biographies of Pocahontas and Helen Keller, Abraham Lincoln and Ronald Reagan. Of Mr. Sullivan, *Publishers Weekly* said, "[he] has mastered the art of writing simply and directly, making complex subjects understandable and interesting." Mr. Sullivan was born in Lowell, Massachusetts, and brought up in Springfield. He now lives in New York City with his wife.

Index